The Boerboel

The Boerboel Dog Owner's Manual

Boerboel dog care, personality, grooming, health, costs and feeding all included
by

Harry Holstone

Dog lover and Mastiff owner

ALL RIGHTS RESERVED. This book contains material protected under International and Federal Copyright Laws and Treaties.

Any unauthorized reprint or use of this material is strictly prohibited. No part of this book may be reproduced or transmitted in any form or by any means, electronic, mechanical or otherwise, including photocopying or recording, or by any information storage and retrieval system without express written permission from the author.

Copyrighted © 2014

Published by: IMB Publishing

Table of Contents

Table of Contents

Table of Contents 3

Foreword 8

Chapter 1: Introduction 12

Chapter 2: Characteristics of a Boerboel 16
    1. Breed Standards 17
    2. Cropping the Ears of a Boerboel 23

Chapter 3: Summary of the Physical Characteristics 27

Chapter 4: The Boerboel and the Bull Mastiff 28

Chapter 5: History of the Boerboel 31

Chapter 6: Personality of the Boerboel 34
    1. Gentle and Calm 34
    2. Loyal Guardian 35
    3. Pecking Order 36
    4. Highly Energetic 39
    5. Endearing Habits 39
    6. Versatility 40
    7. Obedience and Agility 41

Chapter 7: Personality Rating for a Boerboel 44

Chapter 8: Extending Your Home to a Boerboel 45
    1. Ask Yourself if You are Prepared 45

Table of Contents

2. Making a Commitment 46

3. Preparing your Home 47

4. Introducing your Puppy to your Family 48

5. Puppy Proofing your Home 49

6. Get Insurance 51

7. First night in your home 55

8. Puppy Problems that you need to address 57

9. Getting a Boerboel 63

    10) Initial days with the resident pet 65

    a) Special priority to the resident pet 67

    b) If your resident pet is a dog 68

    c) What to watch out for 70

    d) If your resident pet is a cat 71

    e) Within Different Environments 72

    f) Loud Noises 73

Chapter 9: Supplies You Need for Your Boerboel 75

1. Crate 75

2. Bedding 77

3. Toys 79

4. The Collar 81

5. The Lead 83

6. Cleaning Material 84

7. Bowls for Food and Water 85

Chapter 10: Daily Care for a Boerboel 86

1. Feeding your Boerboel 86

2. Free Feeding v/s Scheduled Feeding 87

3. What to Feed my Boerboel? 89

Table of Contents

4. Feeding tips for a Boerboel 94

5. Poisonous Foods 95

6. Poisonous Household Plants 101

7. Poison Proof Your Home 107

8. Garden Plants 107

9. Why Does My Dog Eat Grass? 108

10. Animal Poison Control Centre 108
    a) USA Poison Emergency 108
    b) UK Poison Emergency 108

Chapter 11: Grooming your Boerboel 109

Chapter 12: Training Your Boerboel 116

1. Housebreaking 117
    a) Housing needs of a Boerboel 119
    b) Take the lead 120
    c) Prepare a schedule 121
    d) Bell Training 122
    e) Kennel Training 123
    f) Exercise Pen Training 124
    g) Puppy Apartment™ Training 125
    h) Free Training 126
    i) Mistakes Happen 128

2. The Effect of Reward, Punishment and Discipline 128

3. Equipment Required for Training 129

4. Basic Commands to Teach your Boerboel 130
    a) Teaching your dog to sit 130
    b) Teaching your Boerboel to stay down 130
    c) Teaching your Boerboel to Stay 131
    d) Teaching your Boerboel to come 132
    e) Teaching the Boerboel to heel 134

5. Hand Signals 135

Table of Contents

    a) Hand signal to Come 135
    b) Hand signal to Sit 136
    c) Hand signal to Stay 137

  6. Simple Tricks... 137
    a) Shake a Paw 138
    b) Roll Over... 138
    c) Sit Pretty... 139

  7. Overheating 140

  8. Weaning the Boerboel from his Food Reward 140

  9. The Need for Obedience Classes 141

  10. Surviving Adolescence 142

  11. The Unruly Adolescent 145

  12. Rewarding Unwanted Behavior 146

  13. Giving Up is Not an Option.. 147

  14. Other Activities for your Boerboel 150

  15. Make Sure He Gets Enough Exercise 151

  16. Electronic Training Devices 152

Chapter 13: Travelling With Your Boerboel.............................. 155

  1) Travelling 155
    a) A simple tag with contact details 158
    b) Micro-Chipping.. 158
    c) Tattooing 159

  2) Finding Your Lost Dog 160

Chapter 14: The Health of Your Boerboel 162

  1. Selecting a Vet for Your Boerboel... 162

  2. Preventive Healthcare for a Boerboel 164

  3. Common Health Problems with a Boerboel 165

  4. Dental Care for Your Boerboel 175

Table of Contents

Chapter 15: Behavioral Problems in the Boerboel **177**

Chapter 16: Showing a Boerboel **183**

Chapter 17: The Cost of Owning a Boerboel **188**

Chapter 18: Caring for Aging Dogs **192**

   1. What to Be Aware Of *192*
      a) Physiological Changes 192
      b) Behavioral Changes 192
      c) Geriatric Dogs 193
      d) More Bathroom Breaks 193

   2. How to Make Them Comfortable *194*
      a) Regular Checkups 194
      b) No Rough Play 194
      c) Mild Exercise 195
      d) Best Quality Food 195
      e) Clean and Parasite Free 195
      f) Plenty of Water 195
      g) Keep Them Warm 195
      h) Indoor Clothing 196
      i) Steps or Stairs 196
      j) Comfortable Bed 196
      k) More Love and Attention 196

   3. What is Euthanasia? *197*

   4. When to Help a Dog Transition *197*

   5. Grieving a Lost Pet *199*

   6. The Rainbow Bridge Poem *200*

Conclusion **202**

Foreword

Dogs are wonderful creatures. They are easily the best 'stress busters' that we could ask for. One thing that every dog lover would agree with is that they can be there for you always, unconditionally. So, it is every dog owner's responsibility to make sure that all the needs of the dog are fulfilled. The first step towards this is to ensure that you know everything that is required for the proper care of your beloved furry friend.

There are several dog breeds that require a great deal of care. These rare breeds are often brought to the rest of the world from a rather specific type of habitat. So, they need special conditions and special care so that they grow to be healthy and content. You definitely do not want to see your wonderful little pet moping around the house, almost seeming lazy and unhappy.

With breeds like Mastiffs and Boerboels, the owners must be very well equipped to bring the dog home. These breeds are very powerful and can get behaviorally violent if they are not taken care of properly. As the owner, you must know how to train your Boerboel and help him/her become a social beast. If you fail to do that, you will be putting yourself and also your guests at a great risk. To begin with, Boerboels are quite intimidating, given their size and their reputation. However, with the right owner, a Boerboel can be the most pleasurable pet to have at home.

If you are reading this book, they you either have a Boerboel at home or you are contemplating bringing one home. I really hope that you are the latter as this book will help you understand whether or not the Boerboel is the right breed for you.

Foreword

With the information that is provided in this book, you will be able to answer the three most common concerns of a pet owner:

- a) Is it safe to have a certain breed at home?
- b) What does the daily care for a certain breed include?
- c) Am I financially and emotionally equipped to keep a breed content?

Important to mention

Please understand that much of the content written in this book can be applied to EVERY dog, because when it comes right down to it, a dog is a dog no matter what size, shape, color, price tag or fancy hybrid name we humans might attribute to them.

Every dog has a uniquely wonderful set of gifts to share with their human counterparts, if only us humans would listen.

They "tell" us when they are unhappy, when they are bored, when they are under-exercised, yet often we do not pay attention, or we just think they are being badly behaved.

However, as previously mentioned, it is highly important that you train a Boerboel dog well, as it can be a dangerous dog if not trained properly and can cause harm to you or others.

Many humans today are deciding to have dogs, instead of children, and then attempting to manipulate their dogs into being small (or large) children. This is having a seriously detrimental effect upon the health and behavior of our canine companions.

In order to be the best guardians for our dogs, we humans need to have a better understanding of what our dogs need from us, rather than what we need from them, so that they can live in safety and harmony within our human environment. Sadly, many of us humans are not well equipped to give our dogs what they really need and that is why there are so many homeless and abandoned dogs.

Foreword

A professional dog whisperer is always challenged with the task of finding amicable solutions for canine/human relationships that have gone bad, once the humans understand what needs to be changed, almost every stressful canine/human relationship can be turned into a happy, forever after.

The sad part is that many humans are simply not willing to do the work and devote the time necessary to ensure that their dog's needs are met. Almost all canine problems are a direct result of ignorance or unwillingness on the part of the canine guardian to learn what the dog truly needs. Forget about the breed for the moment, because what the dog needs to be a happy and well-balanced family member has nothing to do with size, shape, color or breed.

First and foremost, our dogs need to be respected for their unique canine qualities. For millennia, the dog has been considered *"Man's best friend"*, and in today's society, when we want to do the best by our canine companions and create a harmonious relationship, we humans need to spend more time receiving the proper training so that we can learn how man can be dog's best friend.

Any dog can be "man's best friend" providing that the human guardian gains the knowledge they need in order to create a happy environment for the dog. While basic training techniques apply to every dog, every dog and every human/dog relationship will be unique.

For this reason, when referring to daily feeding, care, house training, behavioral training, socializing, etc., these chapters are not written to apply specifically to the a certain breed, as this information can be applied equally successfully to any dog.

It is absolutely true that *"With the proper training, Man can learn to be dog's best friend."*

Foreword

I hope that you enjoy reading this book as much as I enjoyed writing it.

Chapter 1: Introduction

Chapter 1: Introduction

The Boerboel is a large dog of the Mastiff breed that hails from South Africa. This wonderful breed is a favorite among dog lovers in South Africa who easily claim that it is the only breed in the world that is bred to be a working dog and a guard dog. Of course, these claims have been met with several disagreements, as there are other large dog breeds such as the English Mastiff and the Bull Mastiff that also have a rather important role to play as a guard dog.

The name "Boerboel" when translated means "The Farmer's Dog". It is true that in South Africa, the Boerboel was strictly created for guarding the homestead. It was in fact one of the only dogs in South Africa that was bred purely for its abilities as a great guard dog.

Even today, the Boerboel is a popular dog among people who have large estates and properties. Because of its large body and agility, the Boerboel makes a very intimidating first line of defense against intruders and also predators. This makes them

Chapter 1: Introduction

very useful on cattle and poultry farms where predators are the biggest threat to the owners.

In the past, the Boerboel was also used to help hunters. They were exceptional in tracking down prey and also at holding down wounded prey. These dogs are renowned for their strength and skill. A Boerboel could single handedly take down large predators like lions, hyenas and all other big cats. If you were to speak to old farmers in South Africa, you could listen to many tales about the strength, skill and agility of this breed.

The best thing about the Boerboel is that it is a family dog. They are known for their strong protective instincts. These dogs will go out of their way to make sure that their family is safe. Of course, this also means that they love hanging around with members of their family. If you have a Boerboel at home, you must make sure that there is someone with him, as much as possible. They can get really upset and sad if they are made to spend long hours without the company of their family.

For those who have owned or interacted with Boerboels, it is common knowledge that it is not a territorial dog per say. While they like to know that they have a territory of their own, they are not very protective about the property that they live in, like the Neapolitan Boerboel. Instead they will focus all their protective instincts towards their family.

The most interesting quality of a Boerboel is that it is instinctively well behaved. These dogs are seldom noisy and difficult to keep at home. All you need to do is ensure that your Boerboel is well bred and really cared for. After that, proper socializing is good enough to have a dog that knows how he/she should behave around people. These dogs have the unique ability of gauging the difference between a threat and a non-threat. That makes them all the more easy to have in your home. It will ensure that he/she does not alert you or bark without any reason.

Another impressive quality of the Boerboel is its agility. Despite the size of the dog, it is quick to respond to disturbances and any

Chapter 1: Introduction

sudden threat to his/her safety. For this reason, he/she is a lot more intimidating than other large guard dogs like the other Mastiffs or descendants of the Boer Dog such as the Bull Mastiff. The Boerboel is a very active dog and only requires good training to make it an impressive, reliable and extremely efficient pet.

Although the Boerboel is not aggressive without reason, they are known to be quite dangerous when they are faced with any hazard to themselves or their family. Additionally, the sheer size of this breed acts a weapon of destruction. Boerboels love people and they tend to get jumpy and excited when they meet new people. So, you must pay a lot of attention to training them to stay down, heel and not jump upon people. Not many are strong enough to withstand the weight of these gentle giants.

These big guys, sadly, are unaware of their size. All they realize is that they love to snuggle up to their human friends or just sprawl around on the floor or the furniture. If your Boerboel has learnt to snuggle up with you at night, make sure you get a bed that is large enough. If it doesn't find any space around you, it will make himself comfortable ON you. Now, that is something that we definitely do not want.

Despite the belief that the Boerboel is dangerous, the most common sights are children and Boerboels playing quite happily. You will see that kids often make their Boerboels comfortable backrests as they complete their homework or read a book. These dogs can be very patient and will not mind being used as a little couch for the kids.

The only important thing with a Boerboel is its upbringing. If you are able to socialize it and be around people from its puppy years, you can be sure that he/she will be very calm and gentle as he/she grows up. These dogs are perfect for almost anyone who is willing to put in some effort to ensure that their pet is happy.

The name is pronounced quite differently across the globe. However, the right way to say it is "burbull". So if you go to a breeder, you know how to ask for a Boerboel puppy without

Chapter 1: Introduction

sounding like someone who has no clue about the breed. Even if you do have no clue, the next chapter will tell you how you can fake your expertise about the breed and ensure that you bring home the right dog.

Chapter 2: Characteristics of a Boerboel

The Boerboel is one of the most recognizable breeds of dogs. It has physical characteristics that are rather unique to the breed and, hence, it is quite easy for you to pick your Boerboel. There are certain physical characteristics that you must look out for when you are bringing home a Boerboel.

According to the Federation Cynologique Internationale, the Boerboel is meant to be a guard dog and a defense dog. It is a breed that is par excellence. Despite the great size, this majestic beast is gifted with the mental balance to be docile and protective at the same time. These dogs are one of the best protectors of people as well as property. The FCI describes the Boerboel as a brachymorph. This means that its trunk is longer that its height. However, the proportion of the physique of this breed is quite harmonious. Even the profile of this gorgeous beast is quite proportionate and visually pleasant.

The most obvious physical feature of the Boerboel is its head. The large head of the Boerboel is known for the characteristic brown mask. Usually, irrespective of the color of your Boerboel, the muzzle and the area between its eyes have a very obvious brown covering. This highlights the squarish and blunt shape of its rather large muzzle. The ears of the Boerboel are also always black in color.

There is only one word that describes a Boerboel aptly and the word is 'massive'. This dog has a stocky body, a large head and really huge bones. Usually, a Boerboel would weigh about 110 pounds or about 60 kilos.

The interesting thing about the Boerboel is that it looks really bulky and huge. However, it is not the tallest amongst the Giant dog breeds. When it is fully grown it can get really heavy. Of course, there is one really nice thing about the Boerboel; it retains its puppyhood for a long time! This means he/she is not

Chapter 2: Characteristics of a Boerboel

completely mature until he/she is three years old. Of course, the Boerboel does attain its complete height by the time he/she is one year old. However, it takes three long years to get to the full weight.

1. Breed Standards

The characteristics of a Boerboel are very specific. Although to most of us just the above features are good enough to make a loving pet at home, there are some other pet owners who are very interested in showing their Boerboels. If you are one of them, they you must be aware of certain breed standards that will qualify your Boerboel for showing.

a. These standards have been set by the Federation Cynologique Internationale, which is a federation of kennel clubs. This federation is based in Thiun, Belgium. When the name of the federation is translated into English it becomes the World Canine Organization. Of course, this name is not commonly used and most people refer to these guidelines as the FCI guidelines.

b. The objective of the FCI is to promote the breeding of purebred dogs like the Boerboel. They have set basic standards to ensure that breeders are producing puppies that have complete functional health. It is also important for the physical features of a dog to match the recommended characteristics for the breed to ensure that the dogs are able to accomplish functions that are expected of the certain breed. For instance, a Boerboel who is not as powerful as recommended by the standards will not be able to play the role of a guard dog as well as a dog that is really up to all the mentioned standards.

c. The FCI also encourages the exchange of information about canines between various member countries. This helps them initiate the organization of various breed exhibitions across the globe. It also provides them with opportunities to understand the requirements to produce healthy specimens.

d. The FCI standards recommended for the Boerboel are as follows:

Chapter 2: Characteristics of a Boerboel

General Appearance: A Boerboel must appear muscular and strong. They are thick set and are of great size. The length of the body must be greater than the height at the withers. The withers refer to the ridge-like formation that you will see at the point where the shoulder blades of the Boerboel meet.

Coat: Now, the coat of your Boerboel is a very important thing. It is the mark of a healthy dog. It is also a great quality in the Boerboel as it determines the grooming needs of your dog. The coat of the Boerboel is usually smooth, dense, and short. It must have a natural shine, which is the sign of a healthy dog. The fur is of uniform length all over the body, so it is much easier to groom in comparison to other dogs. All you need to do is give your Boerboel a good wash and he/she is good to go. Of course, it will need other kinds of grooming which we will get to in the following chapters.

Do Boerboels shed a lot of fur? Not usually, however, there are seasonal woes that you must prepare yourself for. In the spring and fall seasons, your Boerboel will leave behind traces of hair wherever it rests (or sprawls). Of course, there is nothing that cannot be cured with a little bit of brushing. During these seasons, all you need to do is regularly brush off the loose hairs so that your home is fur- free. You can also use a shedding blade along with a sisal mitt to remove the dead hair from the surface.

Almost all shades of brown, fawn and red are acceptable for the dog. These dogs may also have white patches on their legs and chest. Usually, these dogs do not have a mask (at least the coat colors that are accepted as per the breed standards do not come with a mask|) If you are not keen on showing your dog, getting one with a black mask is a great idea. Brindling or tiny stripes are allowed in almost any color. If your dog's total white area exceeds 33% of his/her total coat color, he/she is not accepted for showing. These dogs are very well pigmented and you will see the pigmentation on the lips, the skin, the palate, and the hair around the eyes, paw pads and toenails. However, paw pads that are pink are considered a fault.

Chapter 2: Characteristics of a Boerboel

Body Proportions: For dogs that are specially meant for showing, the proportions are extremely important. The length of the body, which is measured from the shoulders to the buttock, should be greater than the height when measured at the withers. The proportion should be 10:9. The chest in the Boerboel is also very deep and the depth should be more than half the height of the dog when measured at the withers. Usually, the dog measures 24 to 27 inches at the withers and a bitch would measure 22 to 25 inches at the withers. One interesting thing about the body of this breed is that they are extremely masculine in the dogs and evidently feminine in the bitches. Of course, neither of them look like they lack form but the characteristics of the gender are very obvious.

Temperament: The Boerboel must be loyal and calm. It must never bite without reason or even be overly aggressive. The primary function of a Boerboel is that of a protector. It must be able to defend the property that it is responsible for and also take care of the inhabitants of the property. As a result, the Boerboel must be extremely steady and loyal. It must also have a noble and majestic demeanor. The body language of the Boerboel should be that of a very vigilant and intelligent dog, rather than sloppy and lazy.

Head and Skull: The most striking quality of a Boerboel is the size of its head. It is enormous. All the facial muscles including the muscles in the cheeks and the temples are highly developed. The skin on the head is not loose except near the mouth where it forms the trademark moderate dewlap. However, you can see wrinkles in the forehead when the dog is in a state of excitement.

The head of a Boerboel has a boxy appearance. No matter what side you look at the head from, it should appear like a trapezium. Width is a matter of great concern when you think of the head of a Boerboel. From every angle the head must appear wide and large.

Chapter 2: Characteristics of a Boerboel

The brows of the Boerboel are gorgeous. They are excellently developed and the furrow in the front is well visible. Although the brows are not very high raised, they do attract a great deal of attention.

The nose of the Boerboel has a trademark large, black nose. When you look from the front, the nostrils look really widely placed. These nostrils are black in color and the septum is exactly perpendicular to the jaw when viewed from the front.

The Muzzle: The muzzle is powerful, deep and broad. Unlike most Mastiffs, the muzzle of the Boerboel is rather short. The muzzle of the Boerboel narrows towards the nose. When you look from the side, the muzzle seems to be parallel to the skull. In its proportions, the muzzle is a little more than 1/3 of the head in length.

The Lips: The lips of the Boerboel are a very important feature. The distinct V shape that is formed at the junction of the upper lips is very important for a show Boerboel. The upper lips are very thick and fleshy. The upper lips of the Boerboel form the lower profile of the muzzle. The lowest part of the muzzle is at the corner of the lips where you can see the mucous membrane quite evidently. You can actually draw a straight line from this lowest point to the outer corner of the eye of a Boerboel, giving the face a trademark geometric appearance.

The Jaws: As mentioned before, the breed standards have been established in order to have fully functioning specimen. Now, if the Boerboel is meant to be a protector, its jaws must be powerful enough to do that. The jaws of the Boerboel are extremely powerful in appearance. They have very strong bones that have perfectly fitted dental arches. The lower jaw is always well developed in width.

The Eyes: The eyes of a Boerboel are medium sized. They are not protruding or receding when you view the face from the front. The eyes are widely placed. Even when the dog is relaxed, the

Chapter 2: Characteristics of a Boerboel

eyes must have a very intelligent expression. The eyelids are placed tightly over the eyes. They have complete pigmentation on the eyelids as well. As for the color of the eyes, it is usually dark brown. Of course, for competitions all other shades of brown are accepted.

The Ears: The ears are droopy when your puppy is brought home. However, some dog owners prefer to have the ears cropped off to make the Boerboel look more alert and ferocious. In comparison with the rest of the body, the ears are rather small, even when they are not cropped. The ears are usually widely placed to give the appearance of a wide skull. They have a triangular shape and are flat in their appearance. These ears are held very close to the cheekbone when they are floppy. In case of a Boerboel with cropped ears, they will form a perfect equilateral triangle.

The Mouth: The teeth are flawlessly white and are quite strongly developed. The Boerboel has a scissor bite dentition, which is one in which the upper incisors of the Boerboel are very closely placed over the lower incisors. However, the projection is not so much that the teeth become visible even when the mouth of the Boerboel is shut.

The Neck: The Neck of the Boerboel is cylindrical in shape. It is short in length but is very thick. Usually, the length of the next is about 28% of the height at the shoulder blades. The neck is very well muscled. It is also blunt in appearance. When you measure the circumference of the neck it is almost equal to the circumference of the head of the Boerboel. The base of the neck is very broad and it merges smoothly into the shoulders. The skin on the neck is fairly loose but is not as abundant as the rest of the Boerboels. The dewlap begins at the end of the neck and hangs down to the chest. In females, the muscles on the neck are not so well defined.

Chapter 2: Characteristics of a Boerboel

The Forequarters: When compared to the size of the body of your Boerboel, the forelegs must look strong and well balanced to take the weight of this huge canine. The most important part of the forelegs is the area from the ground to the elbow. When you look at this part from the side or from the front, it should look completely vertical. This means that the elbow is in line with the body. The bone structure should be well developed and must appear extremely strong. The bones of the legs are large and the pasterns are slightly sloping when you look from the profile view.

Needless to say, the shoulders make for a very important part of the Boerboel's body. When measured from a vertical place, the shoulders are placed at a 45-degree angle. The muscles in the shoulders are very strong and are highly developed. The definition of the shoulder muscles is also a very important feature of the Boerboel.

The front feet are quite large and have toes that are very close knit. The pads below the feet are supple but well developed. The pigmentation of the pads is also very prominent and is a contrast to the skin tone of the Boerboel. The nails are also very well defined. They are dark, curved and very strong.

The Hindquarters: Just like the forelegs, even the hind legs are judged as per their ability to balance the entire massive structure of the dog. For this they must look sturdy and powerful. The hind legs have another important role to play. They must provide the right amount of propulsion to enable the dog to run and chase.

The hindquarters are very strong and are extremely muscular. What makes the hindquarters look great is the formation of the second thigh. Usually the hock joint is short and is at an angle. When the Boerboel is standing upright, the hind legs are set wide apart and are set squarely when the dog is standing straight. The hind legs are slightly longer than the forelegs. When the dog is standing, the feet of the hindquarters must point straight forwards. The feet are also slightly larger than the feet of the forequarters.

Chapter 2: Characteristics of a Boerboel

Gait: The gait is a very important trait in every breed of dog. With a majestic breed like the Boerboel, it is still more important as your dog must look like he/she is in complete control. The gait of a Boerboel is the ultimate test in shows. The Boerboel is one of the most agile Mollosers. As for the walk, the gait should be like a lion, quite feline, in fact. What this means is that the dog must be very light on its feet when walking. When trotting or pacing, he/she should resemble a bear. That means, even with the massive body, your Boerboel must look agile and powerful. A good trotting gait is one in which the hindquarter has ample thrust to push into the forequarters. Basically, it should have a very smooth take off. As the speed of the gait increases, the neck will drop a little, making the top line seem inclined forward. In addition, its legs should converge right under the body towards the centre. Whether walking or running, the back must be held firmly.

The Tail: The tail of the Boerboel is set high. The tail is long enough to reach the hocks. Sometimes, the tail may fall a little below the hock joint as well. This is acceptable. The tail has a typical tapering shape. It starts off quite thick at the roots and becomes thin towards the end. When the dog is relaxed, the tail may be hanging down straight. However, in a state of excitement, the tail must be carried at the same level as the back. Curving or curling is not acceptable for a Boerboel.

2. Cropping the Ears of a Boerboel

When discussing the physical traits of a Boerboel, we must speak in more detail about cropping the ears of the dog. While several animal rights activists consider it an act of cruelty, there are many pet owners across the globe that opt for this cosmetic procedure to make their pets more aesthetic to look at. According to many breeders and pet owners, cropping is essential to give a breed it's distinct and trademark appearance. For instance, picture a Doberman without a cropped tail and ears. Now, it is your personal choice to have the ears of your Boerboel cropped, or not.

Chapter 2: Characteristics of a Boerboel

However, if you do chose to do so, you must be aware of the procedure and its consequences to make the right decision.

Cropping through the ages

Cropping the ear has been customary practice for a Boerboel. Studies related to artworks that are thousands of years old containing images of the Boerboel show that the ears of the dog were cropped. In those days, the ears of the Boerboel were cropped in order to make them suitable for fights. A hanging and floppy ear could be ripped off quite easily by an opponent, causing severe damage to the dog's health. Of course, the dog would be defeated in the fight, as well.

Today, cropping the ear is a completely cosmetic procedure. Pet owners who are interested in showing their Boerboel opt for cropping. There are some arguments that cropping the ear is also done for health purposes. They believe ears that are cropped are less prone to infections and problems.

How does cropping change the appearance of the Boerboel?

The only problem with the regular ears of a Boerboel is that it makes the dog look rather lazy and slow. So, when these dogs are entered in shows, it is necessary to make them look alert. For this reason the ears of a Boerboel are cropped. Additionally, the Boerboel has certain functions that require it to look powerful. When the ears are cropped, the Boerboel looks less vulnerable and hence keeps trespassers at bay.

Styles of ear cropping

Depending upon the size of the ear after it is cropped, there are two styles. This is common for any breed that requires cropping of the ears. The first style is known as the "pet" style. This is when the ear is completely cropped off. The second style is known as the "show style" where a little bit of the ear is left intact to give the ear an upright and alert position. You must always look for an experienced vet to help your Boerboel. Amateurs

Chapter 2: Characteristics of a Boerboel

might give the dog an ugly triangular cut that just does not work for your dog in the actual market. Another thing that you must keep in mind is that there are chances of the cropped ears looking uneven although they are the same in terms of the measurement. This is because the texture of the pinnae might be different for each ear.

How the ears are cropped?

The ears are cropped surgically. Usually a brace is used to keep the ear standing upright so that the dog looks alert. These braces are made of cardboard and other similar materials to ensure that the ear is in place while it is developing.

It is recommended that the surgery is done when the Boerboel is still a puppy. These are the developing years when the cartilage of the ear is still in its formative stage. So placing the brace will set the ear in place completely. The time frame that you have to get the ear cropped is rather small. Your Boerboel must be old enough to take the surgical procedure. If the puppy is too delicate, you always run the risk of infections and also complications in the procedure. At the same time, the puppy must also be young enough so that the cartilage is not completely formed. The best time to get the ears of the Boerboel cropped is between 6 and 12 weeks of age. It is ideal if your Boerboel is 8 weeks old.

The amount of cartilage present in the ear does not change when you opt for cropping. When the puppies are born, there is a leathery flap that extends out. It is only this flap that gets cut in order to reduce the length of the Boerboel's ears. If you make a short cut in the ear, the time taken for it to set and stand in an upright position is not much. On the other hand, if you are opting for the long cut, the procedure is a little more time consuming.

Chapter 2: Characteristics of a Boerboel

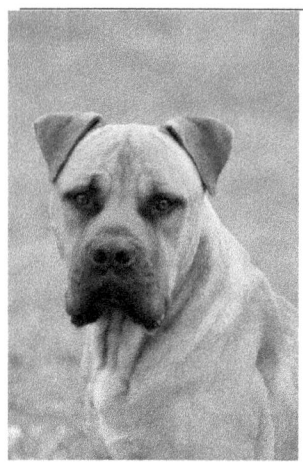

Cost

The cost of the crop depends entirely upon the breed of the dog. Another factor that determines the cost is the type of cropping that you opt for. In this case, the length of the crop and the amount of support that it requires to set in place comes into the picture.

If you are opting for a special sow crop, be prepared to shell out more money. This type of cropping requires an expert. Your local vet will not be able to provide you with the precision that is required to have the ears cropped.

The cropping process is not complex. The surgery does not lead to any complications. However, it is the supplies, the anesthesia, the facilities and the expertise that you end up paying for. The cost of the ear crop will be anything between $200 and $500. That is between 100 to 250 pounds.

Remember, if you notice any infections, rush your Boerboel to a vet. You must also make sure you follow up with your vet on a regular basis.

Chapter 3: Summary of the Physical Characteristics

Weight in the Male-   50- 70 lbs/ 25- 35 kilos

Weight in the Female- 40-50 lbs / 20 to 25 kilos

Eye Color-   Dark brown and all shades of brown

Life Span- 8 to 10 years

Attention Demand- High

Shedding of Fur – Seasonal, usually in spring and fall

Length of Fur- Short, not more that 1.5 cm

Texture of Coat – Dense, smooth and shiny

Color- Brown, Fawn, dark red

Allergenic Property – Moderate

Grooming Needs- Moderate

Associations that recognize the breed- FCI, KC, AKC, ANKC, CKC, NZKC & UKC.

Prevalence of the Breed- Common

Banned in: Some states in the USA

Chapter 4: The Boerboel and the Bull Mastiff

The Bull Mastiff and the Boerboel are so similar in their appearance that it is difficult for a novice to really know what breed he/she is bringing home. If you are particular about bringing home a Boerboel, here are some differences that you must look out for:

Difference between the breeds

- The History of the Breeds: Both the Bull Mastiff and the Boerboel are Mollosers by origin. There are also no records of which breeds were involved in the creation of these breeds and therefore there are no real records of the origins of both breeds. The only distinction in the history of these breeds is their area of origin. While the Bull Mastiff is believed to have originated in England, the Boerboel is a dog of South African descent.

- Size: To the normal eye, it does not seem like there is a size difference between a Boerboel and Bull Mastiff. Especially when you look from the side, these two dogs look almost identical. The Boerboel looks like an athletic version of the Bull Mastiff. However, it is much smaller in size than the Bull Mastiff. An adult Boerboel might grow to an average height of about 25 inches while the Bull Mastiff goes up to 28 inches. Even in weight, the Boerboel weighs almost half as much as the Bull Mastiff. While the Bull Mastiff may reach an average weight of about 100 pounds or 50 kilos, a Boerboel is about 50 pounds or 25 kilos in weight.

Chapter 4: The Boerboel and the Bull Mastiff

- Appearance: This is where most dog lovers get thrown off. The Bull Mastiff and the Boerboel are strikingly similar in their appearance. The only difference is their difference in size. Another difference is the mask. For Boerboels that are accepted in shows, masks are not accepted. However, a Bull Mastiff will always have a very obvious black mask.

- Texture of the coat: The coat on the Boerboel is smoother in comparison to the Bull Mastiff. Both the dogs are shorthaired. The density of the hair on the bodies on these dogs also varies largely. Usually a Boerboel will have less dense hair in comparison to a Bull Mastiff. Shedding of the fur is slightly more in the case of a Bull Mastiff.

- Life Expectancy: A Bull Mastiff, like most giant dogs, has a short life span. It has a life expectancy of about 8 to 10 years. On the other hand, the Boerboel lives longer than the Bull Mastiff; for about 10 to 12 years.

- Nicknames: Both dogs have interesting nicknames. Usually, a Boerboel goes by the names of Dogue, the Farmer's Dog or the Boer Dog while the Bull Mastiff is called a Bully.

- Attack Plan: It is no doubt that the Bull Mastiff and the Boerboel are excellent guard dogs. However, the way they attack a person who is a threat is extremely different. A Boerboel is more aggressive. It will instantly attack and bite the person whom it sees as a threat. On the other hand, a Bull Mastiff will simply lock its jaws around the trespasser and will get a good hold on him/her instead of simply attacking them and allowing them even the slightest chance of escape.

Chapter 4: The Boerboel and the Bull Mastiff

Similarities between the two breeds:

There are some obvious similarities between these two breeds. To begin with, one is the descendant of the other. So they are genetically quite similar.

The temperament of both the dogs is strikingly similar. They are both great work dogs that also make excellent companions. Both the breeds are highly reliable when it comes to safeguarding the house or the property. They are highly vigilant and alert and will keep you informed about all the activities that are taking place in your home. If you are looking for a dog that will be loyal and even-tempered, you may choose either breed. The one thing that you must positively remember with these dogs is that they are both pack dogs. So when you bring them home, your family is their pack. These dogs will only listen to the 'leader' of the pack. You must always keep that hierarchy if you do not want your Boerboel to take over and become very stubborn and highly dominating. If this occurs, you will not be able to maintain your control over your dog.

The Boerboel and the Bull Mastiff are quite easy to maintain. They do not shed their skin too much and require minimum grooming, like simple brushing to keep them pleasant on the eyes. These dogs are also quite bulky, although the Bull Mastiff is significantly smaller than the Boerboel.

Both the Boerboel and the Bull Mastiff are considered to be working dogs. Most owners use them as protectors. These dogs are also highly trainable, making it a pleasure to have them at home. They also love to play and hang around with their human companions.

When you are purchasing a Boerboel puppy, which is rather expensive, be sure to ask the breeder for all the possible information to ensure that you are bringing the right breed home.

Chapter 5: History of the Boerboel

The Boerboel has a long and interesting history that many dog breeders have tried to trace and understand. This breed is supposed to be older than the Bulldog and the Bull Mastiff. However, some breeders have a theory that the Boerboel and other Mastiff breeds were being created simultaneously. Some breeders vouch that the Bull Mastiff is the predecessor of the Boerboel while others argue that the Bulldog was used in different breeding lines to create the Boerboel.

It is believed by most breeders that the Boerboel was the result of interbreeding between several native African dogs. These breeds were believed to have been introduced in South Africa by French, British and Dutch settlers who brought these dogs along with them.

However, there are several others who believe that the history of this breed dates longer than that. They believe that the real credit for bringing this breed to Africa goes to Assurbanipal, the Assyrian King. He was the last and one of the strongest kings of the Neo–Assyrian Empire. When he conquered Egypt, several Assyrian dogs were brought into Africa with him. Then they were exported and spread all over the world. These dogs, as depicted in antique Assyrian relics, have features that are strikingly similar to the Boerboel as we know the breed today.

The credit for popularizing the breed goes to Alexander the Great, who took the breed to almost all the lands that he conquered back then. That is how this breed became popular and widespread in Europe. Then, with growing interest in the breed, several ancient breeders created dogs that had a specific temperament. As this process continued, the breed was divided into two varieties of working dogs; the Mastiffs and the Hounds. The Mastiffs were meant to guard people and property, while the Hounds were meant for hunting. These dogs look very similar in their build and

Chapter 5: History of the Boerboel

their appearance. The basic difference lies in their skill and the purpose that they were bred for.

The most important person in the history of the Boerboel is Jan van Riebeeck. When he came to South Africa in 1652, he brought a large dog with him in order to protect himself and his family in an unknown land. This dog was known as a "bullenbitjer". He was a large dog who was extremely mastiff-like in his appearance and his temperament.

After that, several such dogs were introduced into the Cape of South Africa after they became popular for their efficiency as guard dogs. At that time, the primary interest of the breeders was to ensure that these dogs were able to survive in the conditions that prevailed in South Africa. For this, they were made extremely hardy. This is the reason why the Boerboel, too, has this amazing quality even today. During those times, there were no medical facilities or veterinary services that were available for these dogs. So, they had to take care of themselves under all conditions.

Then between 1835 and 1836, the Groot Trek or the Great Trek occurred in Africa. This is when most of the Dutch-speaking colonists were moved towards the centre of South Africa. The purpose of this shift was to help these colonists establish a homeland of their own, without the interference of the British colonists. By this time, all the desirable features of the Boerboel had been established. The old drawings that are available from this era showcase the recognizable breed. After this period, the Boerboels were interbred. Only the dogs that were the strongest and the hardiest of all the bloodlines that existed were able to survive. These dogs were bred to be versatile. They had to be friends to all the family members as well as great working and guardian dogs.

In the year 1983, the Boerboel Breeders Association was established. This association was created in the Senekal district with the primary objective of promoting this breed as a dog that

Chapter 5: History of the Boerboel

was unique to South Africa. Today, breeding the Boerboel is a popular hobby and also a lucrative industry in South Africa.

Chapter 6: Personality of the Boerboel

Knowing the personality of a certain breed is helpful in two ways: Firstly, you understand whether the dog that you are planning to bring home is suitable for your family and home environment. Secondly, it also helps you be prepared to deal with certain requirements of breeds like the Boerboel.

Over the years, a dog like the Boerboel has undergone a lot of changes in terms of temperament. It is a wonder that this dog is perceived as a cuddly companion today. A few centuries ago, it would have probably been the last thing you want lying on your sofa. As the Boerboel breed was crossed with other giant breeds to increase the numbers, they underwent a drastic change in their personality. Today the temperament that breeders have achieved is perfect to make it the best companion and watchdog that you can imagine. Breeders have tried their best to maintain this temperament for the breed as it made the functionality of the breed better. So, when you are bringing home a Boerboel, you must be prepared for a dog who simple loves to be around you, a dog who doesn't know how big it is and a dog who will, literally, slobber you with love. Here are some traits that are unique to the Boerboel:

1. Gentle and Calm

The Boerboel looks like a ferocious beast, especially when its ears have been cropped off. It also has the reputation of being a dog that was used in fights and hunts. Therefore, many believe that the Boerboel is a very ferocious animal to bring home.

The truth is quite contrary and the Boerboel is really one of the gentlest beasts you could ever think of. However, they are protective and can get aggressive when they see any signs of danger. It is absolutely necessary to train and socialize this dog well, as a Boerboel will never attack anyone without any reason.

Chapter 6: Personality of the Boerboel

They will not even show traces of irritation even when they are amongst lot of people, if you have trained them to be social.

Socializing a Boerboel is the first step towards ensuring that he/she behaves well with your guests and visitors. There are several owners who believe that making a Boerboel social will reduce its capacity as a good guard dog. This is completely false as the Boerboel is a highly sensitive creature. It will sense the difference between an individual who is trespassing and an individual who is your friend or acquaintance if he/sje is adequately socialized.

Remember, the Boerboel is a highly vigilant fellow. So it will make it a point to observe everything about strangers and other unwanted visitors thoroughly before it decides to attack.

2. Loyal Guardian

The loyalty of a Boerboel can never be questioned, especially when you consider the gruesome past where several dogs were massacred for their loyalty to their owners during the Second World War. A Boerboel is so protective of people that it lives with, it will take it as his/her personal responsibility to keep them safe.

Like all large dogs, the Boerboels are also pets that require a lot of attention from the owners. So, they get quite attached to the people who take care of them. This trait has been a part of their lives for centuries now and cannot be changed very easily. In fact, if you decide to move or shift, your Boerboel might even resist it because of the love that it develops for its home. Keeping all this in mind, there is no need to doubt the loyalty of your Boerboel.

The Boerboel's world revolves around its master. The person who is in charge of it means the world to a Boerboel. If you gave the Boerboel a choice, he/she would pick spending time with his/her master over anything else. This also shows that the Boerboel seeks some sort of companionship. However, it does prefer

Chapter 6: Personality of the Boerboel

having its master around in comparison to having another canine or animal companion.

Many people still view the Boerboel as a status symbol and will just keep it tied up in the yard. If you intend to do the same, then do not bring home a Boerboel. It will punish you for negligence. Of course, he/she will not pounce on you or try to harm you, he/she will just dig up massive holes around the resting area in the yard. The most difficult thing to manage is a bored Boerboel. It will try to explore whatever is around and will call out to you in scary, low pitched barks. If you are up for dealing with that, you may consider ignoring your Boerboel.

The Boerboel has unique ways of showing love for you. When you are home, it will follow you around. It loves to be a part of your daily life and will be inquisitive about what you are doing. Of course, it also wants you to play with it! So, if you are taking the day off and just watching a couple of movies and lounging around, your Boerboel will wait by your feet eager to play or go out for a stroll when you decide to get off that couch. It will watch you closely and will get excited at your every move.

So, you see, no matter what anyone tells you, know that your Boerboel is loyal to a fault. All you need to do to gain its trust is shower it with some kind words and it will remain loyal for a lifetime.

3. Pecking Order

The Boerboel is known for its unique soft mouth quality. This gives it the ability to carry delicate and small creatures like squirrels in its mouth without causing them any damage. So if you have tiny people or creatures in your home, danger from the Boerboel is the least of your concerns. It will never attack or be aggressive towards resident pets, if used to them. It will also adjust to new pets if introduced correctly. In general, the Boerboel is compatible with most people and animals in your home, as long as they are not strangers who are a threat.

Chapter 6: Personality of the Boerboel

Like any pet that you would bring home, you must also consider the pecking order of the Boerboel. Sure, it is a gentle dog who is seldom aggressive. However, you must never underestimate the primeval instincts of any pet that you bring home. Yes, there are several people who have other pets and also children at home and still manage to keep the Boerboel. However, it does take a good understanding of the dog's psychology to make this happen. If you are not sure of how to handle your children and the Boerboel or other pets and the Boerboel, here are a few tips.

To begin with, remember that it is never ever a good idea to have a child alone with a dog; the Boerboel or any other breed. Make sure you have some supervision when the Boerboel and a baby are interacting with one another. The Boerboel is very tolerant towards children and makes a great couch and backrest for the kids. However, that does not mean that it is meant to entertain your child. It will not be too pleased if your child constantly teases or bothers the dog. Remember, the Boerboel is programmed to attack when threatened. Therefore, if there is a kid in the picture, you should always make the child aware of the fact that the dog is not a toy.

The Boerboel is a dog that requires a commanding master, whether it is an adult or a child. Now, a Boerboel is pretty gentle towards human children and will never hurt them on purpose. However, the size of the Boerboel is also a threat to the well being of a child. Sometimes, in their excitement, Boerboels may knock over and even step on children and hence harm the child. So, it is best that you are around when your child is with the Boerboel.

When it comes to other pets, the Boerboel is tolerant towards them as long as it gets to be the boss. If you have another dog that is an alpha by nature, you must reconsider bringing home a Boerboel. They never get along with another animal that wants mastery over their territory. For instance, if you have two Boerboels of the same gender in your household, you must consider separating them and reducing the severity of the disagreements that they might have. If you have a female and a male, on the other hand, the male will allow himself to be subdued while the female takes over. There are some cases when the female and male will also fight for an alpha position. So, if you are housing Boerboels at home, it is best that you keep them away from each other.

With smaller animals, you are just putting them at risk with a Boerboel. These dogs love to chase creatures that are smaller than them. Of course, you can control the interactions and supervise, but you can never control the outcome of unsupervised interactions between your Boerboel and the other smaller animals that you have at home.

In conclusion, the Boerboel's pecking order is as follows:

1. Kids
2. Other dogs
3. Smaller animals like cats

That being said, try to avoid unsupervised interactions at all times.

4. Highly Energetic

A Boerboel has loads of energy. Most often, they like to let this energy out by chasing. Their favorite chasing targets are cyclists and vehicles. Boerboels also enjoy chasing a small and fast animal like a cat or rabbit. This makes it important for the owners to be very careful to ensure that the Boerboel does not cause any damage to other animals and people. The dog must also be protected as chasing vehicles and cycles might lead to severe accidents.

A Boerboel must be trained to be obedient to avoid bad behavior. Training does not involve punishing or reprimanding your dog for bad behavior. The best thing to do with a Boerboel is to appreciate it when he/she behaves in a manner that is acceptable to you. They are very quick to learn the difference between what is socially acceptable and what is not.

As the owner, you must be in charge at all times. It is best if there is one consistent master who will command the Boerboel. This is an obligation that you have towards the Boerboel as its owner. If you cannot take this charge, you must reconsider bringing it home. The most important thing that you need to do as the owner is channel its energy in the right direction. If your dog is given ample exercise, it will not indulge in practices like chasing too often.

5. Endearing Habits

There are some things about your Boerboel that will just make you grow fond of it with each passing day. Chewing is one such habit that is common with the Boerboels. This might be a matter of concern to most people who are worried about the belongings that the Boerboel might happily chew into bits. Of course, you need not worry about this as the Boerboel can be trained to chew only toys and large bones to fulfill the need to chew things.

Chapter 6: Personality of the Boerboel

Another habit of the Boerboel that you cannot ignore is drooling. Now, drooling is more of a natural process than a real 'habit' in case of a Boerboel. These dogs have a very loose and thick muzzle that falls over the upper lip. So, when the dogs eat or drink, they tend to drool a lot. Another thing that comes into mind is the size of the animal. Most people believe that drooling is a cooling mechanism of sorts as far as the Boerboel goes. Remember that a dog as large as the Boerboel requires a lot of food. So, if you are going to have a Boerboel at home, be prepared for a lot of drooling. The drool is thick and has almost the same consistency as egg whites. If the Boerboel is drooling at all times, even when there is no food or water involved, you must raise your concerns. This means that the Boerboel is either stressed, scared or even unable to handle high temperature. You must then take adequate measures to make your Boerboel feel comfortable and safe.

The last habit that I would like to mention is snoring. This is a habit that is not exclusive to a Boerboel. All Boerboels indicate that they are sound asleep by snoring loudly. Even if your Boerboel is sound asleep on the first floor, you will be able to hear its loud snores in the ground floor. Now, if you are a light sleeper, you might want to buy yourself a pair of earplugs.

6. Versatility

A dog like the Boerboel is an excellent choice because of its versatility of function. This breed makes for a great companion and also ensures that your home is well guarded and taken care of. The temperament of this dog is ideal as it helps you find a great companion in it. There is a dilemma that the Boerboel is often confronted with. To begin with, it is a compulsive work dog. It takes the role as the guardian of the house extremely seriously. This is instinctive and you cannot remove this trait from the dog.

The Boerboel will fulfill its duties as a guard dog while being a great companion. The appearance of the dog itself makes it very formidable. It has the head of a gargoyle and the body of a looming beast. With just these qualities it is able to keep intruders at bay. Now, for those who take a look at the Boerboel, it seems like a lazy dog that is just lounging around. However, what most people don't know is that a Boerboel is never in a state of inertia. It could just be resting or even sleeping but it will act instantly when it expects some danger to the property or family.

The Boerboel always tries to save energy for when it actually requires it. So you will see it resting and lounging a lot. It is even tempered and is very calm at most times. The important thing to know about a Boerboel is that it will wait, watch and then attack if necessary. These dogs are not like the German Shepherds or the other breeds that like to patrol. They will have a watchful eye on their home and property while they cuddle up on the couch or just wait by your feet.

7. Obedience and Agility

It seems almost unfair to expect agility of a Boerboel. However, despite its large size, the Boerboel is an extremely agile dog. It loves to play, run and even jump. In fact, the Boerboel is the most agile among the Mastiff dogs. Its movement is always very free flowing and smooth. However, these large dogs also require their share of rest to ensure that their limbs do not get too exerted. The advantage for the Boerboel is that it is very muscular and despite its size, it is not a very heavy dog. However, it will not appreciate it when you force him/her into going on a jog with or just run alongside a bicycle.

These dogs do not have too much stamina and will begin to drool when they are physically strained too much. Your Boerboel will love the outdoors and will also play fetch, but at its own pace. Never try to rush the Boerboel on the pretext of getting it good exercise, fresh air etc. One thing that the Boerboels love to do is swim. They enjoy their time in the water and will appreciate it if you take them swimming as often as you can. The water will also give them a break from the large weight that they need to carry

Chapter 6: Personality of the Boerboel

around all day. When you force a Boerboel to exercise or do more that what its body is capable of, you can put it at the risk of overheating. This may result in cardiac issues or other conditions that might be fatal.

Remember, if you have a Boerboel puppy at home, you must never over exercise it. This reduces the development of their limbs and also puts their skeletal structure at the risk of permanent damage. If you have a Boerboel puppy, you must only take it for short walks. However, the usage of stairs should be limited. The reason you need to be so careful with the Boerboel is that they have a very high tolerance for pain. Due to this, their injuries often go unnoticed. You will see obvious signs and symptoms only when the condition is extreme.

Obedience is another thing that you can expect from the Boerboel. However, you cannot expect it to obey your command as quickly as breeds like the Aussies and the Shepherds. Whenever you give your Boerboel any command, it will wait, think about it and then react. Sometimes, it seems as if he/she is questioning your command itself. This was a big issue with people who wanted to include their Boerboels in shows. The obedience judges often marked them very low as they seemed to not understand the commands at all. However, with increased knowledge about the breed and its behavior, this perception is soon changing and the Boerboel is receiving better marks for obedience skills.

The Boerboel is a spectacular breed. It is a majestic animal that is very aware that its master is in command. This makes you a lot more responsible for your Boerboel. Most people treat their Boerboel as a working dog and leave it on a large farm with tons of food and water. This is just wrong, as these breeds require a lot of emotional reassurance. Sure, they are powerful and meant for hunts and fights but they tend to get very lonely and confused when they do not have a master.

Chapter 6: Personality of the Boerboel

Human company is very important for this breed, as they have become accustomed to being around people and obeying them for centuries now. If you feel like you do not have it in you to spend time with the Boerboel, you must never attempt to raise one. As most pet owners would agree, this is true for any pet. If you are a first time pet owner, especially, the Boerboel is not a good breed to bring home. You must have some experience with large dogs before you bring home a Boerboel. You must have all the knowledge that you might need to take care of this breed and also keep it happy and content.

Chapter 7: Personality Rating for a Boerboel

To make it easier for you to judge if the Boerboel is the right breed for you, here is a quick rating of the breed. I have marked the most important qualities out of 5 to make sure that you understand how compatible you and the Boerboel will be:

- Affection towards Owner- 5/5

- Aggression - 4/5

- Obedience - 4/5

- Functionality - 5/5

- Adaptability - 4/5

- Playfulness - 4/5

- Compatibility with dogs - 2/5

- Compatibility with children - 3/5

- Compatibility with smaller animals -3/5

- Intelligence - 5/5

- Activity level - 4/5

Chapter 8: Extending Your Home to a Boerboel

When you are bringing a Boerboel home, there are many things that you must do to make the house comfortable for it. Your preparations for bringing your Boerboel home begin from the stage when you collect as much information as you might require about this breed. It is a great idea for you to share this information with other residents of your home before you decide to extend your home to a puppy.

1. Ask Yourself if You are Prepared

Although the Boerboel seems like an excellent breed to bring home, you will have to really reason with yourself whether you are a suitable owner or not. Many dog owners get carried away by the appearance and majesty of the breed without considering many important factors when they bring home a Boerboel puppy. Here are a few questions that you should ask yourself when you decide to bring home a Boerboel:

- Do you have the time to make a commitment and be a full time owner to the Boerboel?
- Is your home large enough to house a Boerboel?
- Does your Boerboel have enough space outside to go on a walk or just lounge around?
- Are there any members in your family, pets and children, who might be put at risk if you bring home a Boerboel?
- Will you be able to afford the care required for a Boerboel?

You see, whenever we decide to bring home a pet, we always believe that we will be able to "walk them everyday", "wash them every week" etc. These commitments cannot be frivolous, as a pure breed like a Boerboel requires you to be a hands on master. Consider your life on a long-term basis when you decide to make that commitment. What if you have to move? What if your schedules change? Are you likely to make drastic changes in your life that might affect the dog? Never make a momentary decision as you are jeopardizing the well being of a beautiful creature.

2. Making a Commitment

Once you decide to bring a Boerboel home, it is a given that you understand your responsibilities towards that dog. It means that you have chosen a Boerboel after carefully studying the behavior and the needs of the breed. This is the breed that fits best into your lifestyle and your requirement, and you are, therefore, making this choice.

When you begin to look for a breeder and actually found one, you are closer towards making your commitment to the breed. You have voluntarily looked for an individual who is responsible towards this breed at a very professional level. If you find a good breeder, you have found someone to help you and your puppy settle down with each other and lead a life together.

I recommend that before you make that commitment, you spend some time with at least one puppy pack. This gives you a chance to study the behavior and personality of each puppy, thereby finding a particular one that best suits your needs. There are several things that you can look for when you are observing a pack of puppies. Some puppies will be evidently outgoing, others will be very quiet and observant. Some of them will display leadership skills that will take you by surprise. So, you can make a wise decision based on what characteristics you require with your puppy. Once you know that a puppy is appealing to you, do not think twice. This is the one you want to bring home.

This time that you spend with a puppy pack does one more thing for you. You will be able to understand the dynamics of a Boerboel and also realize that it is, in fact, not the right breed for you, if this is the case. It is best to come to this realization before you bring a Boerboel home.

If you have friends who have a Boerboel at home, you might also want to spend some time with the adult dogs to understand how easy or complex it is to have a Boerboel at home. Once you are sure, you can make that leap of commitment and bring home your very own bouncy little Boerboel!

3. Preparing your Home

Imagine if you were bringing home a newborn baby. There would be several things that you would take care of before the baby arrives. You will need toys; a crib and other supplies that will help you take care of your baby. A Boerboel puppy too is just like a baby that is covered in loose and wrinkled fur. There is a lot of preparation required in your home and for your family to bring home a special breed like the Boerboel.

The one thing that you must remember is that the Boerboel puppy is coming in to a space that is going to become its home as well. So, the types of preparations that you will make depend entirely on what you expect of the dog. At all times, you are in charge, so you will not bring a puppy into your home and simply let it take over. For instance, if you are bringing home a Boerboel to be a strict working dog, the bedding and the space that it will use will be entirely different from a Boerboel that is brought home for companionship.

While you are limiting the space that the Boerboel can use and the freedom that it will have in your home, be careful to ensure that it does not feel claustrophobic in your home. Space and warmth are the two most essential things that you must ensure for your Boerboel. Of course, I am not talking about warmth in terms of temperature. Your puppy is going through a major transition because it is leaving a home that it is already used to, to make another space its home. It is taken away from the warmth and comfort of its mother and littermates to live among completely new beings.

So, as the owner, it is your responsibility to make sure that you do not deprive the dog of anything. There are many supplies that are mandatory when you bring home a Boerboel. You must also try your best to ensure that it does not feel traumatized. One good idea is to ask your breeder to give you a toy that the puppy is fond of. There must be some form of familiarity that will help your puppy get accustomed to a new place.

Treat the Boerboel like a baby and avoid everything that you would avoid with a child. That is when you will gain the confidence and love of your Boerboel. The good news is that most of the Boerboel puppies are well mannered and even-tempered by nature, which makes it a lot easier on the owners to make this new member in the family feel welcomed and extremely comfortable.

4. Introducing your Puppy to your Family

The idea of bringing a puppy home is very exciting for anyone. The members in your family, especially the kids, will want to pet the dog, play with it and even cuddle. This can be uncomfortable for the puppy as the sights, sounds and sensations of your home are completely new. Here are some ground rules that you must establish when you are bringing a Boerboel home to your family:

Chapter 8: Extending your Home to a Boerboel

- The introduction should be low key. Remember that your puppy is extremely anxious, as it has been brought away from its mother and the breeder who are familiar to it. If you smother it with affection, you will actually drive it away from you and frighten it.

- Human contact is necessary but must be controlled and gentle in the beginning. The puppy will whine and cry a lot. So you must be able to console it. Just let it be and speak to it in a soft voice.

- Do not turn the music or television on too loudly when the puppy is new to your home. This will frighten it out of its wits and make the whole experience of coming into your home traumatic.

- There will be no guests or friends visiting it until it is entirely comfortable. Of course, socializing is necessary for the Boerboel, but you must try you best to not overwhelm it.

- Allow it to explore the place without any disturbance. Unlike pets like cats, your Boerboel does not require any confinement or separate room to get used to the new environment. All it needs to do is sniff around and get used to the common sights and sounds in your home.

5. Puppy Proofing your Home

Yes, there is such a thing as puppy proofing your place. While you are busy making your home comfortable for your Boerboel, you may forget to make the home secure for it. There are several areas in your home that might be dangerous for your puppy. You may also have some regular habits like spraying cockroach spray or using rodent kill to keep your home free from pests. These are things you must reconsider before you bring home a puppy.

The first thing to do before you bring home a puppy is to ensure that you take the necessary precautions that will prevent the

Chapter 8: Extending your Home to a Boerboel

puppy from getting into things that you do not want him/her to get into. If you know that there are objects that might threaten the safety of your puppy, keep them closed or make all the arrangements to make sure puppy is unable to reach them.

Remember that a puppy will be inquisitive. It will investigate, sniff and even chew objects that seem new and interesting. So another reason for you to puppy proof your home is to ensure that none of your belongings are ruined in the process. For instance, if you have breakable objects that the puppy might knock over, you should make sure that they are away from the reach of the puppy. At the same time you must not restrict a full run of your little one.

There are some things that cannot be put away. For instance, consider the electrical cords. While they are potentially dangerous for the dog, you cannot do without them. In such cases, you might consider tying up the wires so that the puppy is unable to get it out and chew it. Of course, you cannot convince or 'train' your puppy to stay away from these cords. The best you can do is not allow it to be dangling around and available easily to the Boerboel.

Even when your puppy is kept in a crate, there is no guarantee that it is entirely safe. Make sure that there aren't any harmful objects like home cleaners or other chemicals around the crate of the puppy. If the puppy is able to reach out with its paw and grab the object or spill it over, you still are putting it in danger.

Drinking out of the toilet water bowl is something that every puppy loves to indulge in. It is your job to keep the lid closed at all times to prevent this. Drinking the water from a toilet bowl might cause harmful infections and severe damage to the puppy's health.

This covers just the inside of your home. You must also ensure that the area outside your home is safe for your puppy, as you cannot restrict it to your home. When the puppy is too young, make it a point to not let the puppy into the outdoors without any

Chapter 8: Extending your Home to a Boerboel

supervision. It should be allowed to walk around the yard and explore while you are watching.

Just because your home is fenced, do not assume that your puppy is safe. The Boerboel is a crafty and persistent creature. If he gets his mind on crossing the fence, he will make a rabbit hole or even jump across if you are not watching. The best thing to do is to make a fence that is really high and well inserted into the ground. For complete protection, the fence must be at least 8 feet high. You must also check that there are no gaps or holes in the fence. It is also important to keep the fence well maintained. Even a small notion that the fence can be crossed will make your puppy persistent to get across. Of course, considering the Boerboel, your puppy may not be attempting to break out or get out of the house. All he is interested in doing is exploring the new space that he is in.

If you have a garden or a yard, you must make sure that there aren't any plants that have very thick and sharp thorns. When the puppy is young, his skin is delicate and he may have serious cuts and wounds if you do not tend and maintain your garden well.

6. Get Insurance

If you are bringing home a special pure breed like the Boerboel, you must make sure that you get your pet completely insured. In some cases, pet insurance is mandatory to get your dog the license that is necessary to have him in the house legally.

Getting pet insurance is equivalent to getting any sort of insurance, be it your own health insurance or car insurance. The idea is to get your dog's health insured so that it can get the right attention when necessary. There are several factors that determine the type of insurance policy that you will get. The premium that you pay on your insurance depends on three things:

- The age of your dog - the older your dog, the higher the premium will be.

Chapter 8: Extending your Home to a Boerboel

- The breed of your dog - the premium that you pay for dogs of a purer breed is higher as these dogs require expensive care and treatment.

- The type of coverage that you require - you must be sure of what you want your policy to cover. The coverage sum is also an important factor for your premium.

With most insurance policies, you should be able to get coverage for injuries due to accidents, common medical problems, poisoning and even severe terminal diseases like cancer. There are some policies that will also cover things like immunization, routine care, flea control prescription, annual checkups and also dental care. Of course these policies are quite expensive and require a higher premium payment.

When you consider the costs of going to the vet and getting your dog checked thoroughly, you will realize that getting insurance is a great thing to do. In an untoward situation when your Boerboel requires attention, you will be able to provide it with all the necessary care and attention without making any compromises.

Most pet owners neglect this rather important step towards pet care. In my personal experience, I have seen that the anxiety and the sorrow that the owners go through in case of medical emergencies is quite traumatic. So, I recommend that you speak to your breeder or even an insurance agent to get the right information about the policies that are available on the market. The best people to give you accurate advice are people who already have pet insurances for their little ones. They will be able to tell you why a certain policy will work and why another will fail.

To begin with, your pup might not be very affectionate and cuddly. Do not jump to conclusions that your pup has a behavior problem. It is just natural that your puppy will like to be by itself for a while. As it becomes more familiar around your home, each

Chapter 8: Extending your Home to a Boerboel

member of the family can take turns to get close to the pup. All you need to do is sit down and get to the level of your puppy. Then allow him to smell your hands, nibble at your fingers or just walk around you, sniffing and contemplating. Doing this on a regular basis will make the Boerboel more relaxed around you.

Dogs are some of the most compatible creatures when they are left with human beings. We all know that. Especially with a breed like the Boerboel who is a full on family dog, you never have to worry about problems in this process. It will eventually get used to you and be playful and happy.

Pet guardians commonly ask themselves, when considering medical insurance for their dog, whether they can afford not to have it. On the one hand, in light of all the new treatments and medications that are now available for our dogs, that usually come with a very high price tag, an increasing number of guardians have decided to add pet insurance to their list of monthly expenses.
On the other hand, some humans believe that placing money into a savings account, in case unforeseen medical treatments are required, makes more sense.

Pet insurance coverage can cost anywhere from $2,000 to $6,000 USD (£1,201 to £3,604) over an average lifespan of a dog, and unless your dog is involved in a serious accident, or contracts a life-threatening disease, you may never need to pay out that much for treatment.

Whether you decide to start a savings account for your dog so that you will always have funds available for unforeseen health issues, or you decide to buy a health insurance plan, most dog lovers will go to any lengths to save the life of their beloved companions. Having access to advanced technological tools and procedures means that our dogs are now being offered treatment options that were once only reserved for humans.

Chapter 8: Extending your Home to a Boerboel

Now, some canine conditions that were once considered fatal are being treated at considerable costs ranging anywhere between $1,000 and $5,000 (£597 and £2,986) and more. However, even in the face of rapidly increasing costs of caring for our dogs, owners purchasing pet insurance remain a small minority.

In an effort to increase the numbers of people buying pet insurance, insurers have teamed with the American Kennel Club and Petco Animal Supplies to offer the insurance, and more than 1,600 companies, such as Office Depot and Google, offer pet insurance coverage to their employees as an optional employee benefit. Even though you might believe that pet insurance will be your savior anytime your dog needs a trip to the vet's office, you really need to be careful when considering an insurance plan, because there are many policies that contain small print excluding certain ages, hereditary or chronic conditions.

Unfortunately, most people don't consider pet insurance when their pets are healthy because buying pet insurance means playing the odds, and unless your dog becomes seriously ill, you end up paying for something that may never happen.

However, just like car insurance, you can't buy it after you've had that accident. Therefore, since many of us, in today's uncertain economy, may be hard pressed to pay a high veterinarian bill, generally speaking, the alternative of paying monthly pet insurance premiums will provide peace of mind and improved veterinarian care for our best friends.

Shop around, because as with all insurance policies, pet insurance policies will vary greatly between companies and the only way to know for certain exactly what sort of coverage you are buying is to be holding a copy of that policy in your hand so that you can clearly read what <u>will</u> and what will <u>not</u> be covered. Don't forget to carefully read the fine print to avoid any nasty surprises, because the time to discover that a certain procedure will not be covered is not when you are in the middle of filing a claim.

Chapter 8: Extending your Home to a Boerboel

Before Purchasing a Policy

There are several considerations to be aware of before choosing to purchase a pet insurance policy, including:

Is your dog required to undergo a physical exam?
Is there a waiting period before the policy becomes active?
What percentage of the bill does the insurance company pay after the deductible?
Are payments limited or capped in any way?
Are there co-pays (costs to you up front)?
Does the plan cover pre-existing conditions?
Does the plan cover chronic or recurring medical problems?
Can you choose any vet or animal hospital to treat your pet?
Are prescription medications covered?
Are you covered when traveling with your pet?
Does the policy pay if your pet is being treated and then dies?

When you love your dog and worry that you may not have the funds to cover an emergency medical situation that could unexpectedly cost thousands, the right pet insurance policy will provide both peace of mind and better health care for your beloved fur friend.
Keep in mind that usually your monthly or yearly premium will increase when your dog gets older.

TIP: Get your pet insurance BEFORE your dog has been to the vet with a health issue. In my case, one of my dogs had something wrong with his eyes and I went to the vet. I took an insurance policy 3 months later and the insurance asked me to give them the pet records. This results that I now have an insurance policy that EXCLUDES anything to do with my dog's eyes.

7. First night in your home

The first night that the Boerboel spends in your home is the most crucial one. Since he has had a rather adventurous day, he might not be entirely comfortable yet. Think of the day from your

Chapter 8: Extending your Home to a Boerboel

Boerboel's point of view. It has come to your home in a car, probably. You must have placed him in the lap of the passenger or in a crate. Usually, Boerboels love to ride in the car. However, the first ride to your place, away from its litter, might not be as pleasant as you expected it to be. Besides crying and wailing, the puppy may also urinate or have loose bowels due to anxiety.

It then goes to the vet, gets a thorough examination. Here, he is amidst several other anxious animals that are dreading their encounter with the vet. Since the Boerboel is sensitive to these vibes, it will be really afraid. If your vet deworms and vaccinates your dog, the poor little guy will be eager to just get back to the breeder.

Then it comes into your home. He/she is adorable and everyone wants to get a piece of the cute little puppy. It will resist this in the beginning but will enjoy it very soon. It will lick the hands of all the members in the house and wag its tail until it realizes that he misses his mom. If it has to meet other pets, especially unhappy cats, it will be a little wary.

After this, he gets to explore the new space around him. It has a new bed, a new yard and other new areas that it has never seen before. It also likes you more since you have probably given him his first meal. It then wanders around, experiencing so many new things that you would expect it to be exhausted.

So, you think it is ready or bed. You leave it on that nice cushion and leave it alone. Now, this is probably his first night entirely by himself. He does not have his littermates around him to cuddle up to. He is scared and lonely and probably cold. So, he will try to grab your attention by whining uncontrollably. It is easy for us to give in and try to simply comfort the puppy or just keep him next to you to stop him from whining.

This is a wrong thing to do, as you will be setting the wrong tone for the rest of the nights in your home. If you keep it with you that night, it will expect that to happen all the time. In addition, on the first night, put your puppy to sleep at about the same time that

Chapter 8: Extending your Home to a Boerboel

you would normally go to bed, unless you want to be up with it until 2 am for the rest of the nights. It is possible to get carried away when it is the first night of your puppy in your home. However, just allow him to get used to the environment and then calm himself down.

If you let your puppy whine and cry for a while, it will eventually fall asleep. Although this is heart rending, be strong and just check on it a couple of times without it realizing that it has your attention. If you succeed in keeping your will strong on the first night, you will be able to help your puppy cope faster.

Of course, there are some things that you can do to help make the first night at your place easier on your Boerboel. Most breeders recommend that you take a piece of the puppy's original bedding along and place it with its new stuff to make it feel like there is something familiar there. If you live in a cold place, you could also put a hot water bottle beneath its bedding. But be sure that it is not able to get his paws on it or else you will have a soaking and very stressed out Boerboel.

8. Puppy Problems that you need to address

There are some habits that you will notice with your Boerboel when he is a puppy. Although in the early stages, you cannot consider these habits as problems, they might affect the behavior of your Boerboel if you ignore them in those years. Just as you consider disciplining a child important, you must also consider disciplining your Boerboel.

There are other reasons why you as the owner have a greater responsibility in doing so. Remember that your Boerboel is a very powerful dog. If you are unable to take proper care of it, you will make it a threat to your guests and even your own family. You must understand that it is a basic need to be able to control a large dog like the Boerboel. For this, you must shower it with attention and discipline in the early years so that it understands who his master is.

Chapter 8: Extending your Home to a Boerboel

Here are some common puppy problems that you must address in order to make sure that your Boerboel grows up to be an elegant and handsome fellow.

Socialization

This is something that you must do right in the beginning. You cannot expect your Boerboel to socialize as effectively even when it is 4 or 5 months old. The moment your puppy gets used to the ambience in your home, you must start the socialization of your Boerboel puppy.

To begin with, socialization is a fine chance to show your Boerboel off to your friends. Now that you have decided to own such a magnificent creature, you must also enjoy some green eyed jealousy that you are bound to be on the receiving end of. After all, your friends are going to wish that the adorable fur ball were in their homes instead of yours. Well, this is just an example from my own life, at the time when I unveiled my Boerboel to my pals. I am sure this is an experience that you will also become familiar with soon.

Now, let's get down to some business and talk in detail about the socialization process itself. The socialization process of your Boerboel begins with the breeder. Once you bring it home, it is your responsibility to continue this process and turn it into a dog that is comfortable in its surroundings. The first 3 months of socialization are the most critical ones.

Drawing parallels with children, again, you must understand that the mind of a Boerboel pup is also a blank slate. The interactions and the experiences that he has in his earliest days help him form an impression of the outside world. It is this learning that will stick with it forever. You see, it is not enough if your puppy is accustomed to your home and family. It must meet other people and also experience new places in the initial stages. If this is not done correctly, there are two things that will happen - it will either become too shy and afraid or it will be excessively aggressive.

Chapter 8: Extending your Home to a Boerboel

In the first three months, you must get as many people to meet it as possible. Avoid interactions with their pets during this time, as your puppy will still not be completely vaccinated. The next socialization phase that you must be very attentive of is between 8 to 10 months of age. This phase is also known as the fear phase. During this time, every interaction that your Boerboel has with the world must be positive and gentle. This is also the time when he is fully vaccinated and will be making his way into the world.

When you get the green light from your vet to take the Boerboel out and allow him to interact with other pets as well, you must spend as much time with him as you possibly can. Include him in all your activities, take him out to cafes that are pet friendly or even fix 'park times' to make him familiar with new people and new experiences. Be very attentive when your pet is interacting with new people, especially children. Any bad experience will make it create a mental response mechanism that will stay with it forever.

Let's assume that your Boerboel met an excited little child for the first time. The kid, in its excitement, ended up manhandling the puppy. Another possibility is that your Boerboel was equally excited and nipped the child too hard. Both situations lead to negative responses. In the first case, your Boerboel feels pain and in the second case, he probably got a sound scolding from you. The result is that your Boerboel will now become afraid of children or will become aggressive towards them. Of course, in the earliest days of socialization, you can still reverse these impressions. However, if this happens in the fear phase, the reversal process can be a lot more challenging.

All the things that your Boerboel learns in the formative years will greatly affect how your Boerboel responds to situations in the future. The more he is petted and handled by people and is made to interact with other animals, the better it is for him. Just make sure that he is supervised at all stages and also that you protect him and reassure him in case negative experiences manage to slip in.

Chapter 8: Extending your Home to a Boerboel

Nipping

When your puppy begins to teethe, it will feel like chewing on things to soothe aching gums. The most common targets for your puppy's teething needs are your fingers. It is adorable when it begins but when the teeth of your puppy make their way through the gums, this nipping can be quite painful.

This behavior must not be curbed. It is a natural progression in your puppy's formative years. So, all you need to do is redirect its attention to other things. To get your puppy to stop chewing on your toes and fingers, the first step is to make it clear to him that it is not cute anymore. Say no in an affirmative voice when he begins to chew or nip at your toes. Sometimes, several no's might be in order to get your puppy to understand that you really mean business. The next step is to replace your finger with a chewing toy.

Using a toy is extremely important, as your puppy needs to comfort himself with some chewing. However, if you fail to redirect his attention, he might even target your favorite shoe or furniture to fulfill his needs. You definitely do not want him to damage your stuff and others' stuff, so buy him loads of chewable toys.

The next step is to tell him what he can chew and what he must not chew. For this, you must respond with a firm no when he is chewing on something that is not meant for him! On the other hand, when you see that he is chewing on the toy, praise him or even give him a treat as a reward. This training mechanism will go a long way in determining how your Boerboel's chewing habits shape up.

When your Boerboel grows up, you must try to get it out of the habit of chewing. You cannot entirely prevent an adult dog from chewing, but you can definitely ensure that it does not damage other things. The most common reason for adult dog chewing is boredom. If your Boerboel is simply lounging around or watching

Chapter 8: Extending your Home to a Boerboel

TV with you, it might want something to chew on. A dog bone is the best thing you can get to help relieve its boredom.

Nipping and chewing must be curbed for safety reasons as well. You, as the owner, might be familiar with your Boerboel's nipping habits. For a child or a stranger this might be a scary thing and if they respond with a scream in fear, your Boerboel might attack them for the sudden response. Also, the nipping of your Boerboel gets more powerful as it grows up. He might never mean any harm but he may also not be fully aware of the power of his bite.

Crying

Now, it is not possible for you to be with your Boerboel at all times. There may be instances when you will have to step out of your home or probably leave him on his own for a while. You may do this only when you think that he is old enough to look after himself without getting too afraid.

If you are out of his range of vision, you can expect you Boerboel to cry and whine. His goal is to grab your attention and make sure that you know that he is around. The last thing the Boerboel wants is to be forgotten by his owner. The whining and crying will be a challenge for you to cope with in the beginning. When you hear your puppy whine, it will simply break your heart. However, it is also necessary for your Boerboel to be able to spend time on his own. That way, when you really have to leave the house or probably go out for work, he will not feel so anxious.

Crying and whining is a response to anxiety that the Boerboel feels in your absence. To make sure he does not hurt himself or get into trouble, you must leave him in the crate in the beginning. Training your Boerboel to like the crate and be comfortable in it is also a part of the 'leaving alone' process. If he feels fully secure and safe inside the crate, he will not stop crying and whining incessantly.

Chapter 8: Extending your Home to a Boerboel

The first step is to make the crate cozy. Add comfortable bedding that is warm and soft. Then, you can leave his favorite toy in the crate to keep him comforted in his perilous time alone. The next step is to make him associate positive experiences with the crate. There are several pet owners who will confine their pet to a crate when it does something naughty. This form of punishment will make the dog associate the crate with negative experiences. So, if you do this and leave the puppy in the crate, it is probably whining as it thinks that it is punished for doing something wrong.

Once the crate is ready, your challenge is to make it feel like it is okay to be on his own for a while. Start placing him in the crate for short periods of time to begin with. In the beginning, he must not be left alone for more than 30 minutes. After that, you may gradually increase the time frame when you see that he is comfortable for this initial duration. Toys will help keep him occupied so that he does not miss you too much.

It is also a good idea to keep him in the crate while you are still in the room for the first few days. That will prevent him from whining and he will also get comfortable in the room. Give him some toys to play with and slowly slip away from the room when he is unaware. If he has not been fussy and noisy while you were away, reward him with a treat.

When you think your puppy is ready to stay by himself for longer time periods, you can still do a few things to be sure that he does not get anxious. You can leave the radio on softly so that the voices of people will trick him into believing that he is not alone. Always leave your puppy in a crate when he is alone. Avoid leashes as they may harm themselves while trying to break free from the leash.

Tackling these puppy problems help in three ways:

- It will tell your puppy who the master is.
- It will make your puppy comfortable with new people and experiences.

Chapter 8: Extending your Home to a Boerboel

- The chances of your puppy growing up to be aggressive or afraid are fewer.

The initial years require a lot of attention and understanding of your puppy's mentality. Unless you are prepared for this, you might not want to bring a Boerboel puppy home.

9. Getting a Boerboel

If you are looking for a Boerboel puppy, there are several places where you can get one. First, you can check with your vet to see if there are any breeders who are specialized in Boerboels. With a breed like this one, you must be assured of its purity. So, you must always look for a breeder who will issue a pedigree certificate for your puppy.

The second step is to check the Internet for puppy sales. If you find someone who you think is reliable, make sure you visit him/her and check out the breeding conditions before you actually invest in a Boerboel.

The last and most recommended step is to check with fellow Boerboel owners. They will be able to put you on to the person they got their puppy from. These people are the most reliable source as they have already been tried and tested.

When you are planning to purchase a Boerboel, make sure you make all the enquiries even if you are at the risk of sounding too pushy. This is an expensive breed to buy and an even more expensive breed to care for if there are unwarranted health issues.

Is it at all possible to adopt a dog as large and challenging as the Boerboel? This is a question worth asking before you get your hands onto something you simply cannot manage. You see, Boerboels are usually single master dogs. So if you are bringing a Boerboel home, you must understand that you are not the master that he is accustomed to. A large dog that is not trained to fit into your lifestyle can be dangerous for you and your family.

Chapter 8: Extending your Home to a Boerboel

However, if you must adopt a Boerboel, there may be some valuable factors that you must consider.

To begin with, you must know where to adopt a Boerboel from. The best place to find out is the Internet, where you can find several genuine shelters and rescue centers where you can get your dog from. These websites also allow you to check specific things like house training and also put in special requests so that you can find a dog that will fit perfectly into your lifestyle. There are also regular "need a home" ads that appear in local newspapers. You can review these ads and make a choice. Today, you also have the option of social media where you can post requests for adoption. There are also several pages on these sites that you can visit and check for Boerboels for adoption. You may even ask your friends and relatives to keep an eye out for these dogs.

You may also check with the experts in your vicinity. The decision to bring home a Boerboel is not an easy one. You must speak to these experts and discuss with them to understand if this is the best choice of dog for you. The experts that you must include in your research are vets, groomers, breeds, walkers and even people who own these dogs. Once you are convinced with the recommendations that you get from your reliable network, you may go ahead and make a decision.

The best place to look for a Boerboel is a breed club. Usually, most breed clubs have rescue groups that are focused on the rescue and treatment of a specific breed. In your case, you can look at Boerboel Clubs. These groups will try to get you the perfect dog to take home to your family.

The problem with regular shelters is that they may hide certain facts pertaining to the dog that you are planning to adopt. You see, dogs that are put in rescue homes are either abandoned, abused or injured. In all cases, the dog has suffered a terrible trauma and must be given special care and attention. If you are unsure of how to take care of the dog, you must definitely not

Chapter 8: Extending your Home to a Boerboel

---

bring him home. That way you are putting his and your life at risk. With breed rescue groups, you will receive all the details of the issues that the dog has. They will also give you tips to take care of the dog. If needed, these breed rescue groups also double as foster homes for your beloved Boerboel.

You must be equipped with all the information about the breed. For this, you must know what to ask the breeder when you decide to adopt a Boerboel. Some vital information for a dog that you want to adopt includes his age, his agility, his ability to mingle with other animals, his house training level, evident displays of aggression including biting and attacking someone and health issues that you must be aware of.

When you have the information that you need and you decide to adopt, you must get a valid contract with your breeder or the rescue group. This document lists certain responsibilities on both ends. Sometimes you may end up with a dog that is impossible to take care of. To avoid this, you can make use of the Internet to understand what conditions are ideal and appropriate for you as the future pet parent. Remember that you are also entitled to certain rights as the person adopting the puppy.

Once you have adopted your Boerboel, make sure you take him to a vet. Whether he is a puppy or an adult, he must be examined thoroughly by a vet to check for obvious health issues. Once your vet has spotted these problems, he/she will be able to give you the appropriate preventive healthcare plan to maintain the health of your Boerboel.

In my personal opinion, adopting a dog like the Boerboel is best for people who have ample experience with a large dog. If you are a first time owner, you must consider a different breed altogether unless you have ample support and experts to help you.

10) Initial days with the resident pet

The first few days of your new dog's interactions with the resident pets is the most crucial period. There are several things

Chapter 8: Extending your Home to a Boerboel

that can go wrong if you allow any negative experiences to creep in when you are just bringing your Boerboel home.

If the pet that you have is a large one, like another Mastiff or even another Boerboel, you must make sure that he stays away from the new puppy. There must be no chance encounter that is unsupervised or unprotected. The best thing to do is to keep your puppy in a confined space until you have the time to make that interaction possible. You may even keep your puppy in a crate and leave him in a common area with the resident pet. Even when your Boerboel is in the crate, he must be able to see you around that space. That will give him a feeling of security. However, if you simply leave him alone in the crate with the resident pet in the room, he might get terrified. This will make him associate the crate with negative experiences, making it very difficult for you to crate train him in the future.

Another simple thing to do is to separate the living areas for the two pets during this initial period. You may even have to move your resident pet's feeding area to a calmer and quieter one to help him escape the sudden introduction of the new puppy. If this is an approach that you opt for, make all the changes well in advance. The resident pet must never feel like you are trying to shun him away and make place for the new pet in your home.

On the other hand, if your resident pet is tiny and is usually in a crate, make sure you leave the crate in the same room as your Boerboel at important times like the feeding hour or even during naptime. This will let the two animals get used to each other while maintaining a safe distance. Encourage your Boerboel to spend as much time near the crate as possible. For this, you can use simple tricks like placing the food bowl or even a favorite toy of your Boerboel close to the crate. While there is no real danger when such interactions are unsupervised, it is recommended that you stay close to comfort either animal if there is any negative reaction. You need not place the crate in the room always. This is an exercise that must be repeated on a regular basis.

Chapter 8: Extending your Home to a Boerboel

Take your puppy everywhere with you and introduce them to many different people of all ages, sizes and ethnicities. This will be easy to do, because most people will automatically be drawn to you when they see you have a puppy because few humans can resist a cute puppy.

Most humans will want to interact with your puppy and if they ask to hold your puppy, this is a good opportunity to socialize your puppy and show them that humans are friendly. Do not let others (especially young children) play roughly with your puppy or squeal at them in a high-pitched voices because this can be very frightening for a young puppy. As well, you do not want to teach your puppy that humans are a source of crazy, excited energy. Be especially careful when introducing your puppy to young children who may accidentally hurt your puppy, because you don't want your dog to become fearful of children as this could lead to aggression issues later on in life. Explain to children that your puppy is very young and that they must be calm and gentle when playing or interacting in any way.

a) Special priority to the resident pet

If there is one thing that pets hate, it is sharing their territory and their master's attention. Usually, most of the negative reaction from the resident pets towards the new puppy is because the new member of the family gets all the attention. It is quite natural as everyone in the house wants to pet the new puppy. They all fuss over him and want to play with him, feed him and simply be around him. No resident pet will appreciate this.

You must understand that this is a very difficult time for the existing pet. So, as the owner, it is your job to make him feel just as special as ever. You may even have to try additional methods to make him the centre of your attention to avoid the development of feelings like anger and jealousy towards the new pet. Here are some simple things that you can do to make this phase comforting for your resident pet:

Chapter 8: Extending your Home to a Boerboel

- Always show your resident pet that he is priority when it comes to feeding. So, if you have scheduled three meals for your new puppy, divide the meal for your resident dog into three portions as well. Try to feed them in the same room. During this time, feed the resident dog first and then provide your new puppy with his meal.

- When it comes to playtime, your resident pet gets to do what he loves most. When you come home after work, greet your resident pet first and then attend to the new pet. The idea is to tell you resident pet that he is just as important as he always was.

- Your new puppy must never be given the chance to push the resident pets aside to get your attention. If you are playing with your new puppy and the resident pet comes to you, attend to him immediately. Talk to him, play with him and pet him immediately. Do not wait until you are done playing with your puppy to attend to your resident pet.

- Dominance is a big issue with resident pets, especially dogs. This is also the reason for most of their fights with the new addition in your family. There are simple gestures that you can follow to make your resident pet feel like he is still the 'senior' pet in the family. A simple example of this is, when you are taking the stairs, make sure your resident pet is allowed to go up first, followed by the new pet.

Although these things seem very trivial and meaningless, to an extent, they mean a lot to your resident pets. If you can follow these tips diligently, you can be sure that your home will be free from fights, jealousy and most importantly,cuts and bruises.

b) If your resident pet is a dog
When you introduce a dog to another dog, the dynamics of that meeting is very different. It is far from what you will experience with smaller pets like cats. There are some precautionary

Chapter 8: Extending your Home to a Boerboel

measures that you must take when you are introducing your Boerboel to a dog:

• Find a time when your resident pet is most calm. This is the time when you can arrange the introductory meeting. The best time is when you have just fed your dog and he is ready for his afternoon lounging.

• Always be in control during these meetings. If your Boerboel is still very young, you must make sure that both the dogs are on a leash. Ask a friend or a member of your family to help you out. Let the other person hold on to the Boerboel on a leash. Then put your resident dog on a loose leash and cautiously approach your new puppy.

• This is a trying time for your dog. So give him many treats for being calm and comfortable around your new puppy. You must focus all your attention on your resident dog, as he is most likely to strike or snap at the new puppy.

• If your dog is friendly and not resentful of the new puppy, you may take them both into your home. This indicates that your resident dog doesn't feel particularly threatened by the new puppy. However, this is also no reason to be negligent. You must still be as vigilant as you were in the initial days until they are both completely used to one another.

• The next thing is to plan the environment inside your home. If you have even the smallest doubts about your dog's reaction when the puppy is brought indoors, make all the necessary arrangements. You can place your puppy inside a play pen or a crate while you continue the interactions between the two pets.

• When two dogs are interacting, never interfere. There is always one of them who is more dominant than the other. While you would mostly expect your resident dog to react violently or negatively, sometimes the reaction of your puppy might surprise

Chapter 8: Extending your Home to a Boerboel

you. Irrespective of which one tries to be intimidating, you must never interfere unless you see potential danger to either one of them. In case of any spurt or outburst, take the side of your resident dog. Remember, you are making a change in his territory. So, it is only natural for him to have that rather dramatic reaction that is solely meant to put the new entrant in his place.

- In case the puppy you are introducing to your new dog is older, you must make sure that they are introduced on a long line. They must be allowed to greet each other while you simply preside or watch over the meeting. The resident dog is the one who gets to lead the new entrant in the family to your house. That gives him a place of authority where he can say, " Welcome to MY home"

Interactions between dogs when thoroughly supervised are usually very easy and simple. However, if your resident dog is very dominating by nature, you may want to put a muzzle on him. If you are uncertain of how to control these meetings, there are several professionals who can help you out.

c) What to watch out for

There are some signs that you must watch out for when you are introducing your Boerboel to a resident dog:

- If your dog wags his tail, it doesn't necessarily mean that he is happy to have the new Boerboel puppy in the house. You must look for other behavior patterns like slight growling, staring and lip curling, which are warning signs. Another important thing to watch out for is the stiffening of the body, which indicates that your dog is not sure of how he must react to the puppy.

- A " play bow" is a common reaction among dogs. This is when the dog keeps his tail high while lowering his forelimbs to the ground. This is a sign that he wants to play and get to know the new dog. This, however, does not mean that the other dog is ready to play too. When you see one dog offer the play bow, you must also look at the reactions of the other dog. If he is not ready, you must not force them to play.

- Indifference is a great behavior for a first time meeting. Either one or both the dogs might be completely indifferent to the interaction. Even this behavior deserves a good deal of praising. You may give your dogs treats, too.

- The most normal behavior pattern is sniffing. If the body of your dogs is relaxed, you have little reason to worry. Encourage them to sniff each other, as it is their way of getting acclimatized to the presence of the other.

- Look for any tension building between the two animals. If you notice even a little tension, call the meeting off. You can reintroduce them on another day or when they have completely calmed down. You can even start by keeping them apart and then reducing the distance as your shower them with praise and of course, treats.

d) If your resident pet is a cat

A cat would be pleased if you just get rid of the new puppy. They see the puppy as this looming creature that is out to get them. Instinctively, cats are intimidated by dogs. If your cat is confident, you have a whole different problem on your hands. A confident cat will allow the puppy to approach it without any hassle. However, it will also be quick to strike your Boerboel on the nose when it feels too threatened. The whole deal here is up to you. Any reaction from your end that is too overwhelming will put your pets on edge. When you are introducing your Boerboel puppy to a cat, here are some pointers that will be of great help:

- The puppy must be kept in an enclosed area with his favorite toy as a distraction. The cat must then be allowed to wander around in the room. One thing to know about cats is that they are very particular about their "free will". If you interfere with their 'free will' you will definitely put the cat off and will ruin the interaction. The only time you will interfere is when the puppy reacts violently to the presence of the cat.

- If the interaction between the two is calm, you can bring the puppy out of the cage and simply place him on a leash while the two animals share their space.

With cats and dogs, there is a chance that they will not be able to get along immediately.
If that happens, all you need to do is keep them in separate enclosures until your Boerboel has been trained to understand the concept of " no" and until you are able to control him with a leash.

e) Within Different Environments

It can be a big mistake not to take the time to introduce your puppy to a wide variety of different environments because when they are not comfortable with different sights and sounds, this could cause them possible trauma later in their adult life.

Be creative and take your puppy everywhere you can imagine when they are young so that no matter where they travel, whether strolling a noisy city sidewalk or along a quiet seashore, they will be equally comfortable.

Don't make the mistake of only taking your puppy into areas where you live and will always travel because they need to also be comfortable visiting areas you might not often visit, such as noisy construction sites, airports or a shopping area across town.

Your puppy needs to see all sorts of sights, sounds and situations so that they will not become fearful should they need to travel with you to any of these areas.

Your puppy will take their cues from you, which means that when you are calm and in control of every situation, they will learn to be the same because they will trust your lead.

Chapter 8: Extending your Home to a Boerboel

For instance, take your puppy to the airport where they can watch people and hear planes landing and taking off.

Take them to a local park where they can see a baseball game, or take them to the local zoo or farm and let them get a close up look at horses, pigs and ducks.

f) Loud Noises
Many dogs can show extreme fear of loud noises, such as fireworks or thunderstorms.

If you take the time to desensitize your dog to these types of noises when they are very young, it will be much easier on them during stormy weather or holidays such as Halloween or New Year's when fireworks are often a part of the festivities.

You can purchase CD's that are a collection of unusual sounds, such as vacuums or hoovers, airplanes, people clapping hands, and more, that you can play while working in your kitchen or relaxing in your living room or lounge.

When you play these sounds and pretend that everything is normal, the next time your puppy or dog hears these types of sounds elsewhere, they will not become upset or agitated because they have learned to ignore them.

Also make sure that you get your young puppy used to the sounds of thunder and fireworks at an early age because these types of shrieking, crashing, banging and popping sounds of fireworks or thunder can be so traumatic and unsettling for many dogs, that sometimes, no matter how much you try to calm your dog, or pretend that everything is fine, there is little you can do.

Some dogs literally lose their minds when they hear the loud popping or screeching noises of fireworks and start running or trying to hide and you cannot communicate with them at all.

Chapter 8: Extending your Home to a Boerboel

Make sure that your dog cannot harm itself trying to escape from these types of noises, and if possible, calmly hold them until they begin to relax.

If your dog loses its mind when it hears these types of noises, simply avoid taking them anywhere near fireworks and if at times when they might hear these noises going off outside, play your inside music or TV louder than you might normally, to help disguise the exterior noise of fireworks or thunder.

As well, some dogs will respond well to wearing a *"ThunderShirt"* which is specifically designed to alleviate anxiety or trauma associated with loud rumbling, popping or banging noises. www.thundershirt.com

The idea behind the design of the ThunderShirt is that the gentle pressure it creates is similar to a hug that, for some dogs, has a calming effect.

Do not underestimate the importance of taking the time to continually (not just when they are puppies) socialize and desensitize your puppy to all manner of sights, sounds individuals and locations because to do so will be teaching them to be a calm and well balanced member of your family that will quietly follow you in every situation.

Chapter 9: Supplies You Need for Your Boerboel

Once you have a puppy at home, there are several things that you will need to keep handy in order to help your puppy get acclimatized to your home and to his new life easily. Some of these supplies are basic necessities when you bring just about any breed of dog home. Here is a quick checklist with tips on how to use them and make them useful for your Boerboel.

1. Crate

You will come across many pet owners and breeders who will shun the use of crates as an act of cruelty. Of course, keeping a dog in a crate all the time is not the right approach. However, the crate itself can be of great help, especially if you are interested in presenting your Boerboel at shows and events. So, if you come across people who look at you with disapproval at the pet store when you are purchasing a crate, you can probably tell them these simple things that make a crate a lifesaver.

Uses of the crate

The puppy crate serves several purposes. Some of them are:

- You can use a crate when you are taking your pet to the vet. Not everybody has another person to accompany them and their pet during their visit to the pet.

- It is a great tool to train your puppy to spend time on its own without feeling afraid or left out.

- You can use your crate to confine your pet in case of injuries. Sometimes, these injuries require your pet to be still or even keep away from people, other animals and even dirt to prevent infections. In such cases, you will find the crate rather useful.

- Often in pet shows, you find yourself waiting for your turn. The best way to keep your pet away from the anxiety backstage is to keep them in a crate with lots of water.

- Crates are very handy when you are travelling with your pet. Whether you are taking your pet in your car or transporting him via airplanes, you will find that crates are very useful.

- Some dogs enjoy sleeping in their crate. If the crate is lined with warm bedding and left open, your Boerboel can go and rest in it whenever he wishes to.

Types of crates

There are basically two types of crates that are available:
- The Fiberglass type
- The Wired Type

The fiberglass type of crate is open in the front and contains wiring. The body of the crate is made from fiberglass. The wired type consists of mesh all around the body of the crate. The type of crate that you invest in depends entirely on the purpose of the crate. There are no real rules for this. Both types of crates offer their own advantages and disadvantages. A wired crate, for instance, is a lot more airy. It lets your dog be aware of what is going on around him. The fiberglass crate is extremely sturdy.

You must, of course, make sure the size is appropriate. A fully-grown Boerboel will need a super sized crate. Your dog must not feel too confined or uncomfortable in the crate in order to be able to spend ample time in the crate. What I recommend is that you invest in an adult dog-sized crate in the very beginning. It is not feasible to buy them again and again as your Boerboel is bound to grow faster than you expect. In addition, crates are expensive and it would be impossible to keep purchasing new ones as your pet continues to grow.

2. Bedding

The bedding that you provide will determine how comfortable and relaxed your puppy will feel in your home. Before I go into the importance of the bedding you provide, let me talk to you a little about the ancestry of your Boerboel. Like all dogs, your Boerboel's ancestors, too, loved to make their own cozy dens. In these dens, the dogs used dried leaves as their preferred bedding material. In the modern times, you cannot really expect to have dried leaves strewn around your home. However, while you think that your Boerboel is far removed from his doggie ancestors, there are some instincts that he holds on to. One such instinct is the need to sleep on a warm bed. So, as the owner, it is your job to keep your dog warm and safe.

Why is bedding important?

This might seem like a redundant question as the bedding is obviously meant for your Boerboel to sleep in. However, the bedding is more important than you think. It is the key to getting your Boerboel acclimatized to your home: Some important functions of the bedding are:

- It gives your Boerboel a warm and comfortable place to sleep in when he is new in your home. Good bedding will reassure him that he is in a safe place.

- Having good bedding will allow your Boerboel to heal faster in case he is injured or unwell. Items like bedding will help him be at ease and hence heal faster.

- Your Boerboel will be emotionally more secure when he has a warm bed to turn to incase he is upset by some event.

- Your Boerboel will be well rested if he has good and clean bedding. Therefore, he will be more energetic and playful.

Choosing the right bedding

Of course, you cannot bring home a bag of dried leaves and keep replacing it. The most suitable bedding for your Boerboel is the crate plate covered with a warm blanket. Here are some tips that will create the perfect bedding for your Boerboel:

- The first bedding that you make must consist of a piece of the bedding that he was used to while he was with the breeder. If you can accomplish that, his anxiety will be reduced.

- Use a fabric that is thick enough to produce ample cushioning so that the dog does not feel the crate plate pressing into his bones.

- The fabric must be still. It should not be too smooth and flowy like satin or silk, as it is very uncomfortable to sleep on.

- The fabric of the bedding must not be rough. Friction between the dog's skin and the fabric can cause irritation and rashes.

- Run your hand over the bedding once when you have laid it. It should be free from bumps and should be completely even for your Boerboel to sleep peacefully.

Once you have taken care of all of the above, you can be sure that your Boerboel has a good bed to rest on. Another responsibility that you have is maintaining the bedding. Especially when your Boerboel is a puppy, he might soil his bedding occasionally. You must wash the bedding immediately and have it replaced. Leaving the bedding unclean will leave an unpleasant smell in your home. Additionally, the bacteria and the germs that thrive on the blanket might lead to unwanted infections. Also ensure that your Boerboel's bedding is in an area where it is free from moisture

Chapter 9: Supplies you Need for Your Boerboel

and dust. This will make the bedding much easier to maintain. It will also ensure that your precious pet is always relaxed.

3. Toys

For any dog to get ample exercise, toys are a must. Of course, walking the dog, taking him for a swim etc are great options. However, toys serve an entirely different purpose when it comes to keeping your dog well exercised and also entertained. No matter what breed of dog you bring home, toys are a must. Just like children, puppies develop several skills when they play with toys.

Uses of toys

Toys have more than one purpose in a dog's life. Here are some benefits of toys that you simply cannot deprive your dog or yourself of:

- Toys are essential in the teething years of your Boerboel. Instinctively, these dogs simply love to chew. So if you do not want your fingers, shoes or any other personal belonging to become the target of your Boerboel's gnaws, make sure you get him toys.

- Toys help keep your pet mentally stimulated. There are some toys that make sounds that your Boerboel will love. It will help keep him active and excited.

- Toys are great for your Boerboel and you to bond with one another. Using these toys to play with your Boerboel will keep you completely entertained as well.

- Toys also help your Boerboel feel comforted and at ease when they are new to your home or when they are troubled by things like vaccinations and illnesses.

Chapter 9: Supplies you Need for Your Boerboel

- They are very useful in helping you train your Boerboel. They act as great tools to generate the desired response from your Boerboel.

- Boerboels get really attached to toys. So these toys ease things like change of homes as dogs associate a sense of familiarity with their toys.

Precautions to take with toys

While toys are great for your Boerboel, they might be hazardous to the health of your Boerboel if proper care is not taken. Here are some simple tips that will help make the use of toys safer for your Boerboels:

- Avoid squeaky toys that have a little squeaker inside. For a dog as powerful as the Boerboel, chances are that your dog will just destroy the squeaky toy in minutes, thanks to his powerful jaws. This is true even for puppies. The squeaker that is present in the toy might choke your puppy if you are not attentive. The best use for a squeaky toy is as training equipment.

- You must never get your Boerboel soft toys either. He will rip it apart in seconds and will probably choke on the stuffing present in the toy.

- Always choose toys that are of good quality. Low costing toys compromise on the quality and use toxic paints to make the toys. These paints might be hazardous for your Boerboel.

- Boerboels love to chew. Sometimes, they will chew their toys to an extent that it begins to fall apart. If your Boerboel's toy is in that condition, you must make sure you get rid of it. If you ignore it, there are chances that your Boerboel will choke on the parts that are falling off.

Choosing toys

There are so many toys that are available on the market that you will definitely get confused when you go out for the first time. Everything looks like great fun for you and your dog. However, you must choose toys that will definitely grab the attention of your dog. There are two things you must keep in mind when you buy toys for your Boerboel. The toys must be durable. Toys like the nylon bone are perfect for your Boerboel. Secondly, this toy must have certain scents and sounds that your Boerboel will enjoy.

4. The Collar

We all know why a collar is important for your Boerboel. The collar is your point of control for a dog as large as the Boerboel. This is where you fix the lead and guide your dog when you are taking him for a walk, holding him back from strangers or keeping him tied when required. The collar is also used for the identification of your dog and usually has details like his name, his license and the address to his home.

There are three basic types of collars that you can use for your Boerboel effectively. These collars have varied functions and are necessary for different stages of your puppy's growth. Of course, you need to make sure that you choose durable and good quality collars for your Boerboel. He is a powerful dog and will require more than a piece of canvas or leather to hold him back as he grows up. So you must use the following types of collars as your Boerboel grows up:

The buckle collar:

This type of collar is ideal for a puppy that is still in his growing years. As the name suggests, this collar comes with a buckle that makes it possible for you to adjust the tightness of the collar. For obvious reasons, this is an extremely important function as far as your Boerboel puppy is concerned.

Chapter 9: Supplies you Need for Your Boerboel

When you put the buckle collar on the neck of your Boerboel puppy, you must check the tightness on a daily basis. It doesn't matter if you loosened it just today, it might get really tight overnight. You know what the consequences will be if you forget to loosen the collar on a regular basis.

You may continue to use this type of collar for everyday use. It is best that you pick up one that is made of nylon or leather, as these materials are most durable. While you can use a buckle collar even on an adult Boerboel, you must have other types of collar that will be able to hold back the power of your Boerboel. You must use a collar that will allow you to control your Boerboel completely in case he goes on a complete aggression spree on your guests, for instance. For this, there are more specialized collars like the ones mentioned below.

The choke collar

This is a type of collar that I am not entirely a fan of. However, it has proved to be extremely useful when it comes to training my dogs. This type of collar is made of steel links that have been attached to each other with a buckle in the end. You can easily slip this collar around the neck of your Boerboel.

The main purpose of this collar is to help you train your dog. The idea is to create enough pressure around his neck to make him uncomfortable. Instinctively, when your Boerboel feels too much pressure around the neck, he will stop pushing through and resisting your training efforts.

This type of collar can also be very dangerous for your Boerboel. It is very easy even for a dog as large as a Boerboel to choke on this type of collar. So, when your Boerboel is out playing or just lounging, you must never have the choke collar on. There are many ignorant pet owners who consider the choke collar a style statement for the dog. Since it makes their Boerboel look more "butch", they prefer to leave it on without paying too much heed to the safety of the poor animal.

Chapter 9: Supplies you Need for Your Boerboel

Remember, a choke collar is a rather cruel thing to use. It is only good when your Boerboel is under your watchful eye.

The halter collar

This is easily the safest and the most humane type of collar that is available. This collar goes over the shoulder blades of your dog rather than his neck. So, it makes it much easier to hold a huge dog like the Boerboel back when you use this type of collar. Using a collar like the halter is best recommended for dogs that are either too difficult to hold back or too tiny to use a choke collar on.

When you have decided what type of collar that you want to use on your Boerboel, you can even have it customized to look more glamorous on your Boerboel. You get several colors that you can choose as per the color of the coat of your dog. You can also have the collar studded with stones and other embellishments if your Boerboel is a girl. Engravings on the collars are also common these days. Today, the collar is more than just another 'supply' for your dog. It is an accessory that you must choose very carefully to glam up your little Boerboel.

You must also use the collar from a young age to ensure that your Boerboel is comfortable wearing the collar on a regular basis. While nylon collars are most reliable, you can choose other materials that you think are strong enough for your Boerboel's power.

5. The Lead

Once you have the collar in place, you will need a lead to make the collar functional. A lead is extremely important to keep your Boerboel in control. The problem with the lead is that it is not good enough to get a lead that is able to hold the strength of your Boerboel back. The lead should also be able to withstand the constant chewing of your Boerboel, especially when he is a puppy. While it is your job to ensure that the chewing habit is redirected towards other toys, there is absolutely nothing that will guarantee that your Boerboel will keep his teeth off the lead.

So, the best type of lead to use would be the one that is made of nylon. These leads serve both purposes and are also quite easy to get. These leads are also very light in weight and are extremely comfortable for daily use. If you are using a nylon lead, you can be assured that it is much easier to put on a puppy that is just being introduced to the concept of leashes. It is light and does not feel like a big addition to the Boerboel's physical space.

When you are getting your Boerboel ready for training, you can switch to a leather lead. This type of lead is great to hold the Boerboel back. However, there is no need to keep the leather lead on at all times. However, it is definitely recommended that you keep a spare leather set handy at all times. You never know when your formidable Boerboel needs a bit of calming down.

6. Cleaning Material

Keeping your Boerboel clean is another important part of your job as a pet parent. We will talk in detain about the actual grooming equipments to keep your Boerboel clean later on. You will need several other things besides the sponges and brushes to keep your Boerboel clean.

When your puppy is still young and in his training stages, you can expect a lot of mess at home on a regular basis. This is especially true when your Boerboel has not been toilet trained. You must keep several old rags and pieces of paper handy to keep your home clean. You will also need cleaning liquids and detergents to really clean up thoroughly. Whatever chemicals you choose for your cleaning kit, make sure that they are pet friendly and free from toxins.

Chapter 9: Supplies you Need for Your Boerboel

7. Bowls for Food and Water

This is perhaps the first thing you will pick up when you bring a pet home. There are two bowls that you will need for your Boerboel. You will require one bowl for food and one bowl for water. Having a single set is not good enough. You will need one set of bowls to keep inside your home and one set of bowls to place outside. It then depends on the Boerboel where he chooses to eat.

You can choose between plastic bowls and stainless steel bowls. The ones made of steel are preferred as they are sterilized and safer to use. Another advantage is that your Boerboel will not chew upon a steel bowl. However, he will completely ruin his bowl if it is made of plastic.

Since the Boerboel is a large dog, you will also need a small stool or stand to place the bowls on. This will keep the food and water closer to the level of the dog and he won't have to stretch too much to eat and drink. This simple facility will also prevent digestive problems like bloating and gastric torsion. He will be able to digest his food easily and, thus, remain healthier.

There are several other supplies that you can include in your list depending upon your lifestyle and the ambience that your puppy will grow up in. You can include several grooming supplies, doggy t-shirts, accessories and even medicines in this list. It all depends completely on what you need the most for your Boerboel to have a happy life. There are several pet stores that you can pick up these supplies from. These days with many more people interested in having pets at home, there might even be a separate aisle for these products in your local super market.

Chapter 10: Daily Care for a Boerboel

You need to take care of several things on a daily basis to maintain the health and well being of your Boerboel. When it comes to a dog like the Boerboel, which is a separate and special breed, you will have to take special care at various stages of his growth to ensure that he is getting everything that he requires to grow into a healthy dog.

1. Feeding your Boerboel

Feeding a Boerboel is very challenging. He is a big dog, so he requires a special diet that is nutritious and suitable for his metabolic needs. Of course, you cannot feed a puppy the same thing that you would feed a Boerboel. I recommend that you read this chapter over a couple of times to understand how you must feed your Boerboel. When you actually step out to pick up some food for your Boerboel, it can be seriously intimidating as there are so many options available, each seemingly better than the other.

Of course, there are various brands of foods that are available. However, if you really look at it, there are three types of foods that are available for dogs: moist food, semi moist food and dry kibble. While most owners simply give their Boerboel dry kibble, as it is the most inexpensive option, it is not good enough to fulfill all the dietary requirements of your Boerboel. A combination of dry kibble with moist food is, undoubtedly, the best thing for your Boerboel. These moist foods consist of almost 70% water and are great for your Boerboel. On the other hand, your Boerboel will absolutely love semi moist food because of the taste and texture. However, with the amount of sugar that these foods contain, I recommend that you never introduce your Boerboel to this type of food at all.

Chapter 10: Daily Care for a Boerboel

As a rule, a Boerboel must be fed at least 2 times a day as an adult and 3 times a day until he is six months old. You must never allow him to be free fed. Free feeding means simply leaving food in his bowl for him to eat when he wants. For a Boerboel, there is no time when he does not feel like he needs food. Feed him on a timely basis for the best results. We will compare free feeding and scheduled feeding for you to understand better.

2. Free Feeding v/s Scheduled Feeding

There are several pet owners who are still debating on which feeding method is better for a dog. Honestly, this depends entirely upon the breed that you have at home. For this book, we will discuss about the types of feeding with the Boerboel in mind.

What is the difference?

This is the basic need, to understand the difference between scheduled feeding and free feeding. Scheduled feeding is when your dog is given a fixed quantity of food at a fixed time. The number of times you feed the dog also depends upon the breed. Free feeding refers to simply leaving the food in the bowl for the dog to eat whenever he wishes to. Many owners opt for this feeding method as they feel satisfied that they are not missing meals because of the busy schedule.

What is best for my Boerboel?

The concept of free feeding relies on the fact that a dog will not be pressured to eat unless he is hungry. This is true for several breeds of dogs. However, with a Boerboel, controlling the amount of food that he consumes is difficult when he is free fed. Boerboels simply love to eat. So as long as there is food in the bowl, he will continue to eat and you will see your dog growing bigger and fatter with each passing day. The last thing you want to do is get a dog that is already that large to become obese.

Chapter 10: Daily Care for a Boerboel

What are the advantages of scheduled feeding?

- You do not have to worry about your dog eating until he is sick or obese.
- You can regulate what your dog is eating, how much he is eating and how often he is eating. That way, you have a direct control over his weight and health.
- Since your dog knows that it is you who decides when to feed him, he will also try consciously to be obedient to you and not upset you, thus, risking his next meal.

Can I go wrong with scheduled feeding?

Well, of course. There are some common mistakes that occur when you opt for scheduled feeding. You may, however, avoid these mistakes with a little bit of planning and information:
- You might forget to feed your dog sometimes.
- The amount of food in each serving might not be enough for the proper development of your Boerboel
- The timing between two meals may be unequal, with some meals being too close and some being too far apart.
- Without proper training, your dog might become a little aggressive during the meal times when he knows his regular feeding timings.

Can the feeding method interfere with training?

There is no real evidence to suggest that free feeding or scheduled feeding have an impact on your dog's training. However, many pet owners and breeders believe that scheduled feeding works best when you are trying to housetrain your dog. Since you are feeding him at a certain time, he will also need to be taken out to relieve himself at a certain time. It is not that free feeding will lead to an undisciplined dog. However, it is certain that free feeding makes it harder for you to train your dog. Another thing that happens with free feeding is that your dog will no longer

Chapter 10: Daily Care for a Boerboel

view food as a reward. Hence, you might not be able to use treats effectively as a reward for performing certain tasks correctly.

3. What to Feed my Boerboel?

Like I mentioned before, there are several beliefs about feeding that vary from one owner to another. Whatever is mentioned in this book is based on my personal experiences with my Mastiffs. For some of you this might seem perfect while there may be some of you who might not find this suitable for your schedule or lifestyle. Irrespective of what you choose to feed your dog, the goal should be to ensure that he gets all the nutrition that he requires.

When you feed your dog only dry kibble, he will require between 4 to 6 pounds or 2 to 4 kilos of dry kibble each day. What works for me is combining dry kibble with home cooked meals. Different types of meats like chicken, mutton or pork can be cooked and mixed with the dry kibble. You may also add vegetables to this mixture to make the food more nutritious. Including a small amount of grains in his meal will also work really well. For this, you may make porridge with bran, wheat, brown rice or even oats and mix it with dry kibble and vegetables. While this is a broad overview of the foods that are suitable for a Boerboel, there are certain specifications that you need to follow with every stage of growth of your Boerboel.

For instance, many of us might believe that feeding a Boerboel a high protein diet is the right thing to do when he is growing. However, after eight weeks of age, you must choose a dry kibble or a diet plan that is rich in carbohydrates and fats instead of proteins. This is because a high protein diet does not allow the skeletal system to form properly. When a Boerboel is given a protein rich diet during the formative years, he will gain mass and grow very rapidly. The proportion of his body mass does not match with his skeletal development, leading to several problems.

Chapter 10: Daily Care for a Boerboel

The food that you choose for your Boerboel has a lot of consequences. It has an impact on his temperament, his coat and also his health. While it is easy to get carried away with what will suit your dog the best, you must first understand the individual requirement of your Boerboel before you proceed to fix a diet for him. You may consult your vet to give you suggestions and help you chalk out an age appropriate plan.

Feeding a puppy

The most obvious food for your Boerboel when he is a puppy is the milk from his dam. It is instinctive for him to begin to suckle from the moment he is born. If you have had a Boerboel puppy birth in your home, you must watch if he suckles or not. If he does not start suckling within half an hour of his birth, you must place him on a nipple that has plenty of milk. When a puppy gets his mother's milk, he will get the most necessary colostrums that will keep him protected for the first eight to ten months of his life.

Undoubtedly, the dam's milk is the best thing for a puppy. However, if your puppy does not feed on the dam's milk, you must feed him yourself. There are several milk formulas that are available on the market. If you do not have enough experience, your veterinarian is the best person to help you give your puppy the best. The thing with feeding a puppy is that it is not good enough to just give him the right quantity of food. You must also choose the right quality of food for your puppy. For the first few days, you must feed your puppy at intervals of two hours.

The first six months are very important for your puppy's feeding. He must be given his dam's milk for at least six weeks after he is born. It is from the third and fourth week that you start introducing him to solid foods. However, there are some breeders and pet owners who believe in providing solid foods earlier to build the puppy into the weaning stage. There are alternate milks and solid foods that are available for your puppy.

It is best to wean your puppy completely from the dam's milk by the time he is seven or eight weeks old. If you are unable to wean

Chapter 10: Daily Care for a Boerboel

him off by this age, it will be difficult to get him to eat the right foods.

There are several junior and puppy foods that are available for your puppy. Be sure to keep the food completely balanced when your Boerboel is in his growing years. Overfeeding him is just as bad as underfeeding him. The puppy must be fed to grow steadily and not too soon, as he will develop skeletal and joint problems when he grows too big for his frame.

Feeding an adult Boerboel

You can give your Boerboel the food necessary for an adult when he is about 3 months old. While a puppy should get not more than 24% of proteins in his diet, you can increase the proportions when your Boerboel is older. When you are making this transition you must definitely consult your vet so that you are able to put your Boerboel on a great maintenance diet.

There are major brands that you can opt for as they specialize in foods for large dogs like the Boerboel. You must check the proportions of several nutrients present in these foods to choose something that is perfect for your Boerboel. You must never simply choose a diet because a fellow Boerboel owner is using a certain diet. Senior and adult dog diets vary as per the dog's body and the circumstances of the dog.

It is great to add some meat into the diet of your Boerboel. Only about 10 % of the total diet should comprise of meat. Your Boerboel will reach complete adulthood when he is about 2 years old. While some dogs mature fully by the time when they are 16 months old, some may take about three and a half years.

Feeding a Senior Boerboel

As your Boerboel grows older, his diet must also change. This is because his metabolism isn't the same as a younger Boerboel. As your dog grows older, the amount of exercise that he gets will also come down significantly. He will also not be able to move as

Chapter 10: Daily Care for a Boerboel

fast as a younger dog. He will also be more sedentary and will sleep for longer periods of time. As his physiology changes, his dietary requirements will also change. You must pay close attention to the development of your Boerboel as the changes in his metabolism and his physiology take place so slowly that they may go unnoticed.

If you continue to feed him a regular adult dog's diet, he will begin to gain weight. This is because he will not be able to metabolize the food as easily as when he was younger. As your dog grows old, he might have developed several health problems that are age dependant. If he is obese, these problems will only increase and become worse if you do not manage his diet properly.

Another change that you will notice is the deterioration of the function of his organs. The kidneys of your dogs will become less efficient and the intestines will not be able to function like before. You can take care of all these age related issues only when you change the diet of your Boerboel with age. Make sure that your dog gets food that he will be able to digest easily. You may also have to reduce the portions of each meal as the dog grows older.

The change in the diet will depend upon your Boerboel's health as he grows older. Sometimes, they require a diet that is extremely light. On the other hand, if your Boerboel is pretty healthy, he will do extremely well even on diets that are premium. Consult your Boerboel's vet on every stage, as he/she is the one who observes how your Boerboel is performing internally as it is growing older.

With the right diet, you will be able to give your Boerboel the perfect amount of vitamins, minerals and other nutrients that are necessary in keeping him healthy and good looking. If you want to present your Boerboel in shows, you might have to take special care to provide supplements that will improve the quality of his foods. However, if you are including these supplements, make sure you check with your Boerboel's vet first.

Chapter 10: Daily Care for a Boerboel

Give him enough water

For a dog as large as the Boerboel, giving him ample water is a must to make sure that his large body has the opportunity to cool off. You must make sure that large amount of clean drinking water is always available for him to drink.

Water is just like all the nutrients that you include in the diet of your Boerboel. In fact, it is probably more important as it helps your Boerboel metabolize and make use of the nutrients that he is obtaining through the diet. Water is also necessary for his organs to function properly. If his body is not well hydrated, his organs might fail and have several problems.

With the Boerboel, it is necessary to change the water in the bowl on a regular basis. This is because the Boerboel tends to leave a lot of slime in the water as he drools while drinking water. You may also require a special towel or cloth to wipe off the excessive food and water that drips and flies around thanks to his terribly loose dewlap. Otherwise, you must be prepared for the drool to be all over you as your Boerboel will come to you any bury his head in your lap immediately after he has had a satisfying meal.

Choosing and storing food

Since there are several types of foods available for dogs, you might find it quite challenging to get the right and the most nutritious food for your Boerboel. There is no fixed proportion to feed your Boerboel. The best way to decide what is right for your Boerboel is to give your dog feeding trials. Ask your vet to recommend the right food groups that you can include in the diet. These trials are dependent upon the weight, activity level and age of your dog. Once you find what is right for your Boerboel, you may continue it for your Boerboel.

You might see that your Boerboel will enjoy certain flavors of food available on the market. While the taste of the food is not really a factor for your Boerboel, he will be interested in the smell of the food. You can store different flavors to keep some novelty in the food that you give your Boerboel.

Once you have purchased the foods that will be suitable for your Boerboel, the next challenge is to ensure that the food is stored well. If you do not keep the foods tightly closed, all the nutrients will escape, rendering the food entirely useless. When you are preparing home cooked meals for your Boerboel, you can be sure of the freshness. However, of you are giving him store bought foods, close them securely and store them in a place where they are free from moisture and dust.

4. Feeding tips for a Boerboel

There are some simple tips that will make it easier for you to feed your Boerboel and ensure that you do not miss out on any of the basics:

- The food that you serve your Boerboel must never be too hot or too cold. Food that is at room temperature is best digested by your Boerboel. Of course, for basic safety reasons you must try to give him food that is maintained at room temperature.

- If you are giving your Boerboel dry food, giving him enough water is a must. You must always serve the food of your Boerboel with a bowl of clean and fresh water.

- Feeding your dog food from the table is not a good idea. You must never give him leftovers from the food that you eat. These foods contain too much seasoning and fats that are not good for your Boerboel.

- Chewing is a great habit for your dog's teeth to develop well. For this reason, giving him dry kibble or even meat chunks is a great idea, as he will have to chew his food well. Giving him soups and stews is not recommended for your dog.

Chapter 10: Daily Care for a Boerboel

- The normal food or your dog must not be changed. This means adding leftovers of your food or mixing in a new commercial food is not good for your Boerboel. These foods add on to the normal diet and break the balance.

- You must change the diet of your Boerboel only for age related reasons. Otherwise, giving him the same food everyday is the right way to go. Dogs don't get bored or sick of the same food over and over again.

With these simple tips, you can be assured that your Boerboel will grow up with all the nutrients that he requires. He will be alert and will be able to function perfectly.

5. Poisonous Foods

While some dogs are smart enough not to want to eat foods that can harm or kill them, other canine companions will eat absolutely anything they can get their teeth into.

As conscientious guardians for our fur friends, it will always be our responsibility to make certain that when we share our homes with a dog, we never leave foods that could be toxic or lethal to them easily within their reach.

While there are many foods that can be toxic to a dog, the following alphabetical list contains some of the more common foods that can seriously harm or even kill our dogs including:

Bread Dough: if your dog eats bread dough, their body heat will cause the dough to rise inside the stomach. As the dough expands during the rising process, alcohol is produced.

Dogs who have eaten bread dough may experience stomach bloating, abdominal pain, vomiting, disorientation and depression. Because bread dough can rise to many times its original size, eating only a small amount will cause a problem for any dog.

Chapter 10: Daily Care for a Boerboel

Broccoli: the toxic ingredient in this food is isothiocynate. If your dog eats broccoli, even though it will not be seriously harmful (unless more than 10% of the dog's normal daily diet is eaten), it will most likely cause stomach upset.

Chocolate: contains theobromine, a chemical that is toxic to dogs in large enough quantities. Chocolate also contains caffeine, which is found in coffee, tea, and certain soft drinks. Different types of chocolate contain different amounts of theobromine and caffeine.

For example, dark chocolate and baking chocolate or cocoa powder contain more of these compounds than milk chocolate does, therefore, a dog would need to eat more milk chocolate in order to become ill.

However, even a few ounces of chocolate can be enough to cause illness or death in a puppy or small dog, therefore, no amount or type of chocolate should be considered safe for a dog to eat.

A dog suffering from having eaten chocolate may display symptoms that include diarrhea, vomiting, increased heart rate, restless behavior, muscle tremors, or seizures. If they have eaten enough of it, they could die within 24 hours of eating.

During many holidays such as Christmas, New Year's, Valentine's, Easter and Halloween, chocolate is often more easily accessible to curious dogs, especially from children who are not so careful with where they might keep their Halloween or Easter egg stash and who are an easy mark for a hungry dog

In some cases, people unwittingly poison their dogs by offering them chocolate as a treat or leaving chocolate cookies or frosted cake easily within licking distance.

Caffeine: beverages containing caffeine, such as soda, tea, coffee, and chocolate, act as a stimulant and can accelerate your dog's heartbeat to a dangerous level. Dogs eating caffeine have been known to have seizures, some of which are fatal.

Cooked Bones: can be extremely hazardous for a dog because when the bones are cooked, they become soft and can splinter when the dog chews on them.

A splintered piece of bone will usually have sharp edges that can easily become stuck in the teeth, puncture the gums, and cause choking if they get caught in the throat. If a sharp piece is swallowed, this could rupture or puncture the intestinal tract or stomach.

Especially dangerous are cooked chicken legs, cooked turkey legs, pork, ham and veal bones. Symptoms of choking include:

Pale or blue gums
Gasping breathing or panting
Pawing or scratching at the face
Slowed, shallow breathing
Collapse and unconsciousness with dilated pupils

Grapes and Raisins: can cause acute (sudden) kidney failure in dogs. While it is not known what the toxic agent is in this fruit, clinical signs can occur within 24 hours of eating these foods and include diarrhea, vomiting and tiredness.

Other signs of illness caused from eating grapes or raisins relate to the eventual shutdown of kidney functioning.

Garlic and Onions: contain chemicals that damage red blood cells by rupturing them so that they lose their ability to carry oxygen effectively, which leave the dog short of oxygen, causing what is called *"hemolytic anemia"*.

Poisoning can occur when a dog eats a large amount of garlic or onions all at once, or when eating repeated meals containing smaller amounts.

Cooking does not reduce the potential toxicity of onions and garlic.

NOTE: fresh, cooked, and/or powdered garlic or onions are commonly found in baby food, which is sometimes given to dogs when they are sick, therefore, be certain to carefully read food labels before feeding to your dog.

Macadamia Nuts: are commonly found in candies and chocolates. Although what causes macadamia nut toxicity is not well understood, the clinical signs in dogs having eaten these nuts may include depression, pale gums, weakness, vomiting, tremors and joint pain, which can occur approximately 12 hours after eating.

Sometimes symptoms can resolve themselves without treatment within 24 to 48 hours, however, keeping a close eye on your dog will be strongly recommended.

Mushrooms: mushroom poisoning can be fatal if certain species of mushrooms are eaten.

The most commonly reported severely toxic species of mushroom in the US is Amanita phalloides (Death Cap mushroom), which is also quite a common species found in most parts of Britain. Other Amanita species are also toxic.

This deadly mushroom is often found growing in grassy or wooded areas near various deciduous and coniferous trees, which mean that if you're out walking with your dog in the woods, they could easily find these mushrooms.

Chapter 10: Daily Care for a Boerboel

Eating them can cause severe liver disease and neurological disorders. If you suspect your dog has eaten these mushrooms, immediately take them to your veterinarian, as the recommended treatment is to induce vomiting and to give activated charcoal. Further treatment for liver disease may also be necessary.

Pits and Seeds: many seeds and pits found in a variety of fruits, including apples, apricots, cherries, pears and plums, contain cyanogenic glycosides that can cause cyanide poisoning in your dog.

The symptoms of cyanide poisoning usually occur within 15-20 minutes to a few hours after eating and symptoms can include initial excitement, followed by rapid respiration rate, salivation, voiding of urine and feces, vomiting, muscle spasm, staggering, and coma before death.

Dogs suffering from cyanide poisoning that live more than 2 hours after onset of symptoms will usually recover.

Raw Salmon or Trout: Salmon Poisoning Disease (SPD) can be a problem for anyone who goes fishing with their dog, or feeds their dog a raw meat diet that includes raw salmon or trout.

When a snail is infected and then is eaten by the fish, as part of the food chain, the dog is exposed when it eats the infected fish.

A sudden onset of symptoms can occur 5-7 days after eating the infected fish. In the acute stages, gastrointestinal symptoms are quite similar to canine parvovirus.

SPD has a mortality rate of up to 90%, can be diagnosed with a fecal sample and is treatable if caught in time.

Prevention is simple, cook all fish before feeding it to your dog and immediately see your veterinarian if you suspect that your dog has eaten raw salmon or trout.

Chapter 10: Daily Care for a Boerboel

Tobacco: all forms of tobacco, including patches, nicotine gum and chewing tobacco can be fatal to dogs if eaten.

Signs of poisoning can appear quite rapidly (within an hour or less) and may include diarrhea, vomiting, a heightened state of activity, excessive salivating and panting.

Depending upon how much a dog may have eaten, more acute signs of poisoning may cause twitching, leading to collapse and coma due to heart attack that will cause death.

Never leave tobacco products within reach of your dog, and be careful not to let them pick up discarded cigarette butts when they are young puppies.
If you suspect your dog has eaten any of these, seek immediate veterinary help.

TIP: when your dog is a very young puppy, use a double leash, collar and harness arrangement, so that you can still teach them to walk on leash with a Martingale collar around their neck, but can also attach the second leash to their harness so that you can easily lift them over enticing cigarette butts or other toxic garbage they may be trying to eat during your walks.

Tomatoes: there is atropine in tomatoes, which can cause tremors, dilated pupils, tremors and an irregular heartbeat in a dog that eats them. The greatest amount of atropine will be found in the stalks and leaves of the tomato plant, next is the green tomato (before it ripens), and then ripe tomatoes.

Xylitol: is a highly used artificial sweetener, which is often an ingredient in candy, gum, breath mints, toothpaste and mouthwash that is recognized by the National Animal Poison Control Center to be a risk to dogs.

When dogs eat products containing Xylitol, it causes a sudden release of insulin, which causes low blood sugar, which can also cause liver damage.

Within 30 minutes after eating a product containing Xylitol, the dog may vomit, appear to be tired, and/or be uncoordinated. However, some signs of toxicity can also be delayed for hours or even for a few days. Xylitol toxicity in dogs can be fatal if left untreated.

Please be aware that the above list is just some of the more common foods that can be toxic or fatal to our fur friends and that there are many other foods we should never be feeding our dogs.

If you have one of those dogs who will happily eat anything that looks or smells even slightly like food, be certain to keep these foods far away from your beloved dog and you'll help them to live a long and healthy life.

6. Poisonous Household Plants

Many common house plants are actually poisonous to our canine companions, and although many dogs simply will ignore house plants, some will attempt to eat anything, especially puppies who want to taste everything in their new world.

More than 700 plant species contain toxins that may harm or be fatal to puppies or dogs, depending on the size of the puppy or dog and how much they may eat. It will be especially important to be aware of household plants that could be toxic when you are sharing your home with a new puppy.

Here is a short list of the more common household plants, what they look like, the different names they are known by, and what symptoms would be apparent if your puppy or dog decides to eat them.

Chapter 10: Daily Care for a Boerboel

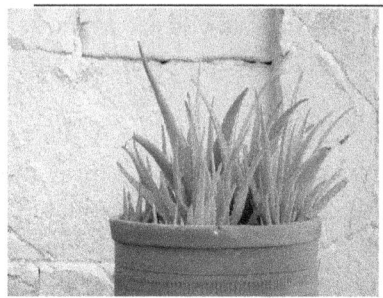

Aloe Plant: also known as *"medicine plant or Barbados aloe"*, is a very common succulent plant that is toxic to dogs. The toxic agent in this plant is Aloin.

This bitter yellow substance is found in most aloe species and may cause vomiting and/or reddish urine.

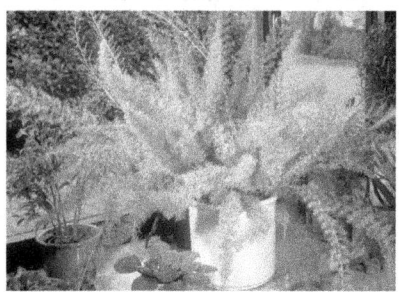

Asparagus Fern: is also known as *"lace fern, emerald fern, emerald feather, sprengeri fern and plumosa fern"*. The toxic agent in this plant is sapogenin, which is a steroid found in a variety of plants. Repeated exposure to the berries of this plant causes vomiting, diarrhea and/or abdominal pain or skin inflammation.

Chapter 10: Daily Care for a Boerboel

Corn Plant: also known as *"ribbon plant, cornstalk plant, dragon tree and dracaena"*, is toxic to dogs. Saponin is the offensive chemical compound found in this plant. If the plant is eaten, vomiting (with or without blood), loss of appetite, depression and/or increased drooling can occur.

Cyclamen: also known as *"Sowbread"*, is a pretty, flowering plant that, if eaten, can cause diarrhea, vomiting and increased salivation. If a dog eats a large amount of the plant's tubers, usually found underneath the soil at the root level, heart rhythm problems can occur, which may result in seizures or even death.

Chapter 10: Daily Care for a Boerboel

Dieffenbachia: also known as *"exotica, dumb cane and tropic snow"* contains a chemical that is a poisonous deterrent to animals. If a dog eats the plant, they will experience mouth irritation, especially on the tongue and lips that can lead to increased drooling, problems swallowing and vomiting.

Elephant Ear: also known as *"cape, caladium, malanga, pai, taro and via sori,"* contains a chemical which is similar to a chemical also found in dieffenbachia. A dog's toxic reaction to elephant ear is similar, including oral irritation, problems swallowing, increased drooling, and vomiting.

Chapter 10: Daily Care for a Boerboel

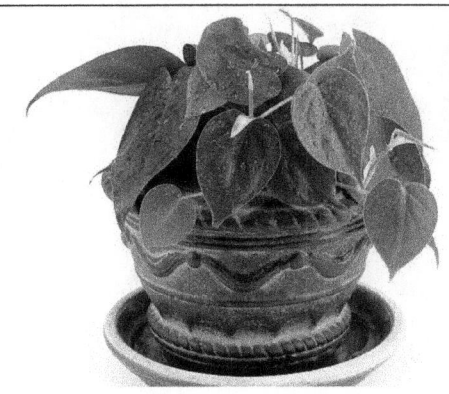

Heartleaf Philodendron: also known as "cordatum, split-leaf philodendron, fiddle leaf, fruit salad plant, horsehead philodendron, panda plant, red emerald, red princess, and saddle leaf", is a very common, easy-to-grow houseplant that contains a chemical irritating to the mouth, tongue and lips of dogs. An affected dog may also experience difficulty swallowing, vomiting and increased drooling.

Jade Plant: has many other names, including "baby jade, Chinese rubber plant, dwarf rubber plant, friendship tree, jade tree, or Japanese rubber plant". While exactly what is toxic to dogs in this plant is unknown, a dog eating a Jade plant can suffer from loss of coordination and depression as well as a slowed heart rate.

Chapter 10: Daily Care for a Boerboel

Lilies: some plants of the lily family can be toxic to dogs. The peace lily (also known as Mauna Loa) is known to be toxic to dogs. Eating the peace lily or calla lily can cause vomiting, irritation to the dog's tongue and lips, problems swallowing and increased drooling.

Satin Pothos: (silk pothos), if eaten by a dog, the plant may cause irritation to the dog's mouth, lips and tongue, while the dog may also experience vomiting, difficulty swallowing and drooling.

The plants noted above are only a few of the more common household plants, and every conscientious dog guardian will want to educate themselves before bringing plants into the home that could be toxic to their canine companions.

Chapter 10: Daily Care for a Boerboel

7. Poison Proof Your Home

You can learn about many potentially toxic and poisonous sources both inside and outside your home by visiting the ASPCA (Animal Poison Control Center) website.

Always keep your veterinarian's emergency number in a place where you can quickly access it, as well as the Emergency Poison Control telephone number, in case you suspect that your dog may have been poisoned.

Knowing what to do if you suspect your dog may have been poisoned and being able to quickly contact the right people could save your dog's life.

If you keep toxic cleaning substances (including fertilizers, vermin or snail poisons and vehicle products) in your home or garage, always keep them behind closed doors.

In addition, keep any medications where your dog can never get to them, and seriously consider eliminating the use of any and all toxic products, for the health of both yourself and your best friend.

8. Garden Plants

Please note that there are also many outdoor plants that can be toxic or poisonous to your dog, therefore, always check what plants are growing in your garden and if any may be harmful, remove them or make certain that your puppy or adult dog cannot eat them.

Cornell University, Department of Animal Science lists many different categories of poisonous plants affecting dogs, including house plants, flower garden plants, vegetable garden plants, plants found in swamps or moist areas, plants found in fields, trees and shrubs, plants found in wooded areas, and ornamental plants.

9. Why Does My Dog Eat Grass?

Be aware that many puppies and adult dogs will eat grass, just because. Perhaps they are curious, bored, or need a little fiber in their diet.

Remember that canines are natural scavengers, always on the lookout for something they can eat, and so long as the grass is healthy and has not been sprayed with toxic chemicals, this should not be a concern.

10. Animal Poison Control Centre

The ASPCA Animal Poison Control Center is staffed 24 hours a day, 365 days a year and is a valuable resource for learning about what plants are toxic and possibly poisonous to your dog.

a) USA Poison Emergency

Call: 1 (888) 426-4435

When calling the Poison Emergency number, your credit card may be charged with a $65 (£39.42) consultation fee.

b) UK Poison Emergency

Call: 0800-213-6680 - Pet Poison Helpline (payable service)

Call: 0300 1234 999 - RSPCA

www.aspca.org   =   ASPCA   Poison   Control.

Chapter 11: Grooming your Boerboel

Grooming your Boerboel is more than just making it look good. You need to groom your dog in order to ensure that it remains healthy and clean. If you ignore the basic grooming rituals, there are several infections that might be on their way. Grooming is also needed to take care of certain safety standards. For instance, clipping the nails is essential to ensure that the Boerboel does not hurt itself or others.

Brushing your Boerboel

Brushing is a routine grooming activity that is essential for your Boerboel's fur. There are several kinds of brushes available on the market that work perfectly on your Boerboel's short and rough hair. Choose a brush that reaches down to the skin of your Boerboel so that it gets a good and thorough brushing.

Brushing is more than just an activity that keeps your Boerboel's fur looking good. It is a very practical grooming routine for several reasons, such as:

- All the dead skin and hair that accumulates on your Boerboel's body is removed. This helps keep the pores unclogged and also prevents the hair from shedding all over your house.

- Brushing the hair with even strokes also improves blood circulation, making it easier for the new skin and fur to grow.

- Brushing is a great opportunity for you to check for bumps and rashes that may go unnoticed when you don't pay attention to the skin of the Boerboel.

- Grooming and brushing the hair is a great way for you to bond with your Boerboel.

Chapter 11: Grooming your Boerboel

Brushing the hair at least twice a week is highly recommended. The short and rough fur of your Boerboel is not exactly high maintenance but a good brushing session impacts the overall hygiene of your dog. Unlike bathing, brushing is an activity that your Boerboel will also enjoy thoroughly. If you use even and smooth strokes to brush your Boerboel's fur it will feel like a day at the spa for your beloved pet.

Bathing

Bathing a dog is something that every pet owner and pet find stressful. The issue with most pets is that they are not given a regular bathing routine from the time they are puppies. If you train your Boerboel to expect a bath after a certain interval you will notice that it will struggle and fuss a lot less.

A dog does not require a bath as often as people. However, a good bath at regular intervals is a must. With dogs like a Boerboel that has so many wrinkles on its body, bathing becomes a lot more necessary. There are several areas where dirt and germs can accumulate and cause serious infections. So you must make sure that you give him a bath that is thorough. Follow the steps below to ensure that your Boerboel is getting the right kind of bath:

- Step 1: Wet the fur of your Boerboel completely. You may use a water hose for a Boerboel that is fully grown.

- Step 2: Use a good dog shampoo and work up lather. Always shampoo the body first, wash it and then proceed to the face. When you are shampooing your Boerboel, make sure that you get the shampoo well into the skin. While you are doing so, be on the lookout for bumps, boils or lesions in the skin.

- Step 3: As mentioned before, rinse the body and wash it thoroughly and wash the shampoo out thoroughly before proceeding to his face. When you wash the face of the Boerboel,

Chapter 11: Grooming your Boerboel

direct the water away from his eyes. If you are washing his forehead, cover his eyes with your hand.

- Step 4: Your Boerboel will start this step for you by shaking off the water vigorously. So after you have rinsed your Boerboel, use a leash or collar to step away from him while still having a firm grip. This prevents your Boerboel from running away. Once he has done his bit, use a large and heavy towel to remove all the excess water. If it is a warm and sunny day, allow his coat to dry naturally. However, if the weather is cold, use a hair dryer.

When you are bathing your Boerboel, there are some safety precautions that you need to take. If you are bathing a puppy, you should use a basin or a tub. Make sure you have a non-slippery surface made of rubber or cement to prevent injuries. Never use shampoo that is meant for human hair. These shampoos are too abrasive and will strip off the essential oils from the skin of the Boerboel. There are specially formulated dog soaps that are available in all pet stores. Your Vet will also be able to provide you with medicated shampoos that are good for your Boerboel's skin. Always make sure that you rinse the fur completely and get rid of all the shampoo. If you leave the shampoo behind, even traces of it, the chemicals in them can lead to skin infections.
Sometimes, your Boerboel may require some spot fixing. In such cases you have dry shampoos and dry bathing products that are available in the form of sprays and powders. Although these are not replacements for a regular bath, you can use them when your Boerboel decides to get a little messy.

When you give your Boerboel a bath, always try to keep him relaxed. Take a lot of time out to give him a bath so that you don't end up rushing things. Talk to him soothingly and give him some of his favorite toys so that he remains distracted. The best thing to do is to make him associate bathing time with fun and other positive emotions right from his first bath.

Chapter 11: Grooming your Boerboel

Cleaning your Boerboel's ears

The ears are the most sensitive part on a dog's head. It is prone to infections that might have serious repercussions on the overall health of your Boerboel. Taking complete care of the ears is your prime responsibility as the owner.
You can use cotton swabs or ear buds to get into the deeper areas of the ear. You need to be very gentle as you may damage the inner ear if you are too rough. There are also special ear wipes that are available in pet stores to clean the ear as well as disinfect it. This is something that I strongly recommend for you to buy and store.

Another problem with the ear is that there may be some growth on the fur on the inside of the ear. If this ear hair is too dense, parasites get an opportunity to hide and infect the area. Using small scissors and clipping the ear hair is strongly recommended for all dogs.

When you are cleaning the ear of a Boerboel, also check the ear for infections. If there is any redness or visible irritation of the skin, you can be sure that it is an infection. Sometimes you can also smell an odd odor coming from the ears. This is a sure shot sign of ear mite infections in the ear. If you also notice that the Boerboel is shaking its head too often or scratching his ears all the time, a thorough ear inspection is necessary.

Clipping the nails

When your dog is just walking down your hallway and you hear an obvious clicking sound coming from his toes, it is a sign that your dogs nail needs clipping. Keeping the nails short makes your Boerboel look smart and well groomed. Besides that, there are three prime reasons for you to include nail clipping as a mandate in your Boerboel's grooming routine:

Chapter 11: Grooming your Boerboel

- If the nails are too long they are at the risk of breaking and bleeding. If the nail breakage is too severe it might lead to limping in your Boerboel.

- Someone might get injured when your Boerboel playfully jumps on them or whacks them with his paw.

- All your sofas, rugs and carpets are at the risk of being damaged.

When you are cutting the nails of a Boerboel, be sensitive to a part known as the "Quick". The Quick is a blood vessel that goes almost up to the tip of your Boerboel's nail. This quick is visible when your dog has light colored nails. However if the nails are dark, you must be extra careful when you are clipping the nails of your Boerboel.

Sometimes it is possible that you accidently clip this Quick. This will lead to profuse bleeding and will be painful for your Boerboel. So whenever you are clipping your Boerboel's nails, keep some cotton and coagulant handy. If you happen to cut the nail too far, don't panic. Just apply some coagulant, stroke your dog and talk to him soothingly. When he has calmed down, proceed to the next nail.

Whenever you are clipping the nails of your Boerboel, make sure you have a firm grip on him. This is especially important for puppies as they may make some quick movement or try to run away, leading to injury.

Always clip the nail little bit at a time. When the nail has reached the size that you are comfortable with, simply file it to keep it well maintained. There are special dog nail clippers that help you cut your Boerboel's nails quickly and safely.

Grooming a dog requires a great a deal of patience. Some activities like nail clipping and ear cleaning require experience. If

Chapter 11: Grooming your Boerboel

you are unsure about them, you can hire dog grooming specialists to help you out and teach you the right way to keep your Boerboel looking good, safely and without any stress. Although these services might be expensive in the beginning, I recommend that you opt for them until you are able to care for your Boerboel on your own.

Essentials for a grooming kit

When you are grooming your Boerboel, you must have all the things that are necessary to complete each grooming activity successfully. You must always update your kit and keep refilling things to ensure that you do not have to run to and fro in the middle of a grooming session. Imagine a situation when you have taken your Boerboel to the garden, wet his coat completely, only to realize that you have run out of shampoo. All you will have is a wet and very displeased dog. To avoid these situations, make sure your grooming kit has the following items:

- A good quality dog shampoo
- Pet hand gloves
- Brushes for the fur
- A dog hose
- Large Towel
- Tissues and wipes
- Cotton
- Blood coagulants
- Flee powder
- Dog nail trimmer
- A pair of small scissors

Chapter 11: Grooming your Boerboel

These are the basics. However, you may add other things to this kit, depending on your Boerboel's requirements.

Chapter 12: Training Your Boerboel

With a dog that is as large as a Boerboel you must make sure that he is well trained. A dog his size is a huge responsibility and if he displays unacceptable behavior you may be putting people around you and yourself at risk. Having a trained dog is also important because it is fun. If you have a dog that can respond the way you want him to it becomes easier to play with him and have a good time with him. Training a dog also gives you an opportunity to understand his communication and respond to it adequately.

If you are experienced with a big dog like a Boerboel, you may train him yourself. However, if this is your first time it is a good idea to join an obedience class. You must teach your dog good manners and understand where some behavioral pattern is coming from. Being able to communicate with your dog is a gift. It helps you understand that your pet is an interesting creature that is smart, well behaved and loads of fun. Training him also a great stress reliever for you. When you see your dog display his devotion to you on a daily basis, it is hugely rewarding. Every time your dog obeys you he treats you not just like a leader but considers you his hero. This works very well for a person's ego.

There are certain patterns that owners and obedience counselors have discovered in training and dog ownership. For instance, irrespective of the breed, the best time to train a dog for maximum results and highest success rate is when he is a puppy. I am sure you have all heard of the saying "you cannot teach an old dog new tricks". This saying is quite literal in its meaning. If you want to exploit your dog's learning capability to its maximum you must ensure that you start right.

The best time to start training the puppy is when he is between 10 to 16 weeks old. During this time your puppy is highly curious and is able to learn about anything you teach him. At this stage you have one big advantage. Your dog is not producing any hormones. So training him ensures the highest success rate. Until his hormones kick in, his level of focus is very high and his point of focus is you. All he knows is that you are his source of food and security.

At this point all he wants to do is follow you from one room to another. He does not want you to be out of sight for even a moment. This is when a Boerboel learns how to respond to other people and animals from you. If you are friendly, he will be friendly. On the other hand, if you are hesitant, he will also be hesitant.

The next stage is when your Boerboel begins to produce hormones. This is when he wants to understand what is around him. He will start investigating and exploring everything he sees. Hence his span of attention is extremely low. He will not be able to focus on you and listen to your commands. If you have not trained him, be prepared for a Boerboel who will simply ignore your commands and wander away.

When you know the time is right, look for obedience classes near you. Sometimes the class may be close to your place but too expensive. If the class is reasonable the travelling time may be too much. So to make it easier for you I have put together certain procedures that will yield positive results. Age is not a barrier if you are patient and if you follow the right techniques of teaching and training. The most important thing to keep in mind is that you must use encouragement, motivation and applause as your biggest strengths while training your Boerboel.

1. Housebreaking

If you don't want to run after your Boerboel with a rag and a broom, house breaking is the first thing you must teach him. It is very important to make it clear to your Boerboel that there are only certain places that are suitable for him to use to relieve himself. In the beginning, when you are just taking your puppy out to public places, he may not be able to understand this

Chapter 12: Training Your Boerboel

command immediately. So until the house breaking is complete, always carry a poop scoop with you to remove the droppings of your canine from public places.

There are two types of training that all dogs go through. One is outdoor training where surfaces like cement and grass are involved. The other is the indoor training, which involves your home. When you begin the house breaking process for your Boerboel, decide where you want him to relieve himself. This place should be permanent. If it is a sand box in your home, make sure that you are sure about it. While sand boxes and indoor training works very well with cats, for any dog, outdoor house breaking is recommended.

For every habit that you need to teach, you must find a voice command that will initiate a habit. Now, if you want your puppy to relieve himself, using commands like "let us go, it's time to go, potty time etc." are commonly used. Every time you take your puppy out, give him the relief command that you choose. When he grows into an adult, his behavior will tell you whether he wants to go or not. If he wags his tail, looks at you intently, runs to the door or shows any other sign of interest it means that he wants to go out.

When he is a puppy, your Boerboel will want to relieve himself after every meal and after every play session. You will usually see him looking around for a place to do his business. When a Boerboel is a puppy the muscles in his urinary and intestinal tracts are not completely developed. Therefore he needs to relieve himself quite frequently. Until he is older, you will have to take him out every hour or after every meal and nap. As he grows older, the number of times he needs to go out will reduce. When he is a mature and healthy adult he will not require more than 5 trips. Here is a simple chart that will tell you how many times your Boerboel needs to go out.

- Up to 14 weeks : 10 times
- 14 to 22 weeks : 8 times

Chapter 12: Training Your Boerboel

- 22 to 32 weeks : 6 times
- Adulthood : 4 times

These numbers tell you the minimum relief sessions that your Boerboel requires. However, depending upon the health and condition of your Boerboel, these numbers may vary.

Generally speaking, while your puppy is still growing, a young puppy can hold it approximately one hour for every month of their age.

This means that if your 2-month-old puppy has been happily snoozing for a couple of hours, as soon as they wake up, they will need to go outside.

Some of the first indications or signs that your puppy needs to be taken outside to relieve themselves will be when you see them:

- Sniffing around
- Circling
- Looking for or approaching the door
- Whining, crying or barking
- Acting agitated

a) Housing needs of a Boerboel

With any puppy that you bring home you must establish some boundaries and take some control. Using different types of housing will teach your Boerboel that there is a certain part of the house that belongs entirely to him while the rest of the house is a space that he shares with you and your family.

To establish this control you must first find an area that you can give to him entirely. This is the place where it will sleep, eat and play. It is best that you choose a room where your family spends a good amount of time. A dog must always feel that he is a part of your family and must frequently hear your voice and see you walking about.

Chapter 12: Training Your Boerboel

In the room that you choose you can place a crate or create a gated corner that will become his territory. No matter what type of enclosure you choose, give size a lot of importance. He must be able to stretch well, play and be comfortable. You must ensure that the space is not so large that he can relieve himself at one end and comfortably rest at the other end. The enclosure must be lined with clean bedding. Make sure that water is always available and that his toys are always at arm's length. One thing you must always keep in mind is that you should never put paper in his relieving area or on the floor while house training. If your puppy understands that you will pick up his droppings when he voids on paper, he will associate every paper with voiding. If your goal is to take your puppy outside, he must be forced to go outside and do his business.

b) Take the lead

When you have a baby in the house you try to teach it your way of life. This is exactly what you must do with your Boerboel. Take the lead and help him develop a lifestyle that fits in with you and your family's lifestyle. Your puppy must know when he should eat, when he should go out and exercise, when he should relieve himself and also when he can play.

Teach your puppy that he must sleep in his enclosure. He must also be trained to stay in his enclosure when your family is preparing for the day or when there is a lot of human activity in your home. When you leave the house, the puppy must know where his area of safety is. Remember that making his enclosure a favorite space for him will also prevent him from damaging your things. Instinctively Boerboel loves to chew. They will chew on everything like shoes, furniture or wires. While chewing on furniture is nothing more than a mere damage of property, chewing a wire may be fatal to your Boerboel. When you get back home and find your favorite shoe chewed into bits, you may reprimand him for this act. Your Boerboel does not even remember chewing on the shoe and will simply associate your coming back home to being punished. If you don't want this to happen, train him to be in his enclosure.

Chapter 12: Training Your Boerboel

Another advantage of giving your Boerboel his own space is that he will be able to watch parties and gatherings without being fed food that may cause unwanted illnesses. He will not be under any stress but will still feel like part of all the fun.

c) Prepare a schedule
Every time you release your puppy from his designated area, finish a play session or give him a meal, take him out to the relief area. As he grows, your puppy will show you signs himself. He will circle around the room, scratch the door or just sniff around. Until he knows to do this, you must prepare a schedule.

Whenever you take him out to the relief area, do not stay there for more than five to six minutes. Return to the house after this time period. If your puppy goes when you take him to the relief area, shower him with praise. On the other hand, if he comes back home and then has an accident, sharply say "no" and take him back to the relief area. Keep him there for a few minutes and come back. Never hit your puppy or scare him if he has an accident. Once you come back home, keep him in his crate and clean up his mess. After that, release him to play. If your puppy repeatedly misses going in his relief area, chances are that your scheduling is wrong or that you do not understand his signs of wanting to go out. It is very important for you to make your puppy understand that going outdoors means relieving himself. When he is trained properly, he will be able to tell the difference between playing and relief time. You must also provide similar scheduling for all activities like eating, napping etc. He must be trained to do all this in his enclosure while he is indoors. You must also teach your puppy to be by himself. He needs to understand that you also have other activities to tend to apart from him.

Crate training is highly important for you to give your puppy a place when you know that he is safe. There is no short cut to crate training and house breaking. There are five things that you must ensure for maximum results:

Chapter 12: Training Your Boerboel

- Frequency
- Consistency
- Control
- Praise
- Supervision

If you can follow these simple steps, you will be able to house train your puppy successfully so that he can be a part of your life style and family.

d) Bell Training

A very easy way to introduce your new puppy to house training is to begin by teaching them how to ring a doorbell whenever they need to go outside.

Ringing a doorbell is not only a convenient alert system for both you and your puppy or dog, your visitors will be most impressed by how smart your dog is.

A further benefit of training your puppy to ring a bell is that you will not have to listen to your puppy or dog whining, barking or howling to be let out, and your door will not become scratched up from their nails.

Unless you prefer to purchase an already manufactured doggy doorbell or system, take a trip to your local novelty store and purchase a small bell that has a nice, loud ring.

Attach the bell to a piece of ribbon or string and hang it from a door handle or tape it to a doorsill near the door where you will be taking your puppy out when they need to relieve themselves. The string will need to be long enough so that your puppy can easily reach the bell with their nose or a paw.

Next, each time you take your puppy out to go potty, say the word *"Out"*, and use their paw or their nose to ring the bell. Praise them for this *"trick"* and immediately take them outside.

Chapter 12: Training Your Boerboel

The only down side to teaching your puppy or dog to ring a bell when they want to go outside, is that even if they don't actually have to go out to relieve themselves, but just want to go outside because they are bored, you will still have to take them out every time they ring the bell.

There are many types and styles of *"gotta go"* commercially manufactured bells you could choose, ranging from the elegant **"Poochie Bells™"** that hang from a doorknob, the simple **"Tell Bell™"** that sits on the floor, or various high tech door chime systems that function much like a doggy intercom system where they push a pad with their paw and it rings a bell. (www.tellbell.com , www.poochie-pets.net) In the UK, these bells are available on www.amazon.co.uk .

Whatever doorbell system you choose for your puppy, once they are trained, this type of an alert system is an easy way to eliminate accidents in the home.

e) Kennel Training
Kennel training is always a good idea for any puppy early in their education, because it can be utilized for many different situations, including keeping them safe while traveling inside a vehicle and being a very helpful tool for house training.

When purchasing a kennel for your puppy, always buy a kennel that will be the correct size for your puppy once they become an adult.
The kennel will be the correct size if an adult dog can stand up and easily turn around inside their kennel.

When you train your puppy to accept sleeping in their own kennel at nighttime, this will also help to accelerate their potty training, because no puppy or dog wants to relieve themselves where they sleep, which means that they will hold their bladder and bowels as long as they possibly can.

Chapter 12: Training Your Boerboel

Always be kind and compassionate and remember that a puppy will be able to hold it approximately one hour for every month of their age.

Generally, a puppy that is three months old will be able to hold it for approximately three hours, unless they just ate a meal or had a big drink of water.

Be watchful and consistent so that you learn your puppy's body language, which will alert you to when it's time for them to go outside.

Presenting them with familiar scents, by taking them to the same spot in the yard or the same street corner, will help to remind and encourage them that they are outside to relieve themselves.

Use a voice cue to remind your puppy why they are outside, such as *"go pee"* and always remember to praise them every time they relieve themselves in the right place so that they quickly understand what you expect of them and will learn to *"go"* on cue.

f) Exercise Pen Training

The exercise pen is a transition from kennel only training and will be helpful for those times when you may have to leave your puppy for more hours than they can reasonably be expected to hold it.

During those times when you must be away from the home for several hours, it's time to introduce your puppy to an exercise pen.

Exercise pens are usually constructed of wire sections that you can put together in whatever shape you desire, and the pen needs to be large enough to hold your puppy's kennel inside one half of the pen, while the other half will be lined with newspapers or pee pads.

Chapter 12: Training Your Boerboel

Place your puppy's food and water dishes next to the kennel and leave the kennel door open, so they can wander in and out whenever they wish, to eat or drink or go to the papers or pads if they need to relieve themselves.

Your puppy will be contained in a small area of your home while you are away and because they are already used to sleeping inside their kennel, they will not want to relieve themselves inside the area where they sleep. Therefore, your puppy will naturally go to the other half of the pen to relieve themselves on the newspapers or pee pads.

This method will help train your puppy to be quickly "paper" trained when you must leave them alone for a few hours.

g) Puppy Apartment™ Training

A similar and more costly alternative, the *Puppy Apartment*™ is a step up from the exercise pen training system that makes the process of crate or pen training even easier on both humans and puppies.

The Puppy Apartment™ works well in a variety of situations, whether you're at home and unable to pay close attention to your puppy's needs, whether you must be away from the home for a few hours or during the evening when everyone is asleep and you don't particularly want to get up at 3:00 a.m. to take your puppy out to go pee.

The Puppy Apartment™ is an innovation that is convenient for both puppy and human alike.

What makes this system so effective is the patent pending dividing wall with a door leading to the other side, all inside the pen.

One side of the Puppy Apartment™ is where the puppy's bed is located and the other side (through the doorway) is the bathroom area that is lined with pee pads.

Chapter 12: Training Your Boerboel

With the bathroom right next door, your puppy or dog can take a bathroom break whenever they wish, without the need to alert family members to let them out.

This one bedroom, one bathroom system, which is a combination of the kennel/training pen, is a great alternative for helping to eliminate the stress of worrying about always keeping a watchful eye on your puppy or getting up during the night to take them outside every few hours to help them avoid making mistakes.

According to Modern Puppies: *"The Puppy Apartment™ takes the MESSY out of paper training, the ODORS AND HASSLES out of artificial grass training, MISSING THE MARK out of potty pad training and HAVING TO HOLD IT out of crate training. House training a puppy has never been faster or easier! The Puppy Apartment™ has taken all the benefits of the most popular potty training methods and combined them into one magical device and potty training system. This device and system has revolutionized how modern puppies are potty trained!"*

Manufactured in the United States, this product ships directly from the California supplier (Modern Puppies).

Pricing of the Puppy Apartment™ begins at $138. USD (£83.37) and is only available online at Modern Puppies.

h) Free Training

If you would rather not confine your young puppy to one or two rooms in your home, and will be allowing them to freely range about your home anywhere they wish during the day, this is considered free training.

When free house training your puppy, you will need to closely watch your puppy's activities all day long so that you can be aware of the *"signs"* that will indicate when they need to go outside to relieve themselves.

Chapter 12: Training Your Boerboel

For instance, circling and sniffing is a sure sign that they are looking for a place to do their business.

Never get upset or scold a puppy for having an accident inside the home, because this will result in teaching your puppy to be afraid of you and to only relieve themselves in secret places or when you're not watching.

If you catch your puppy making a mistake, all that is necessary is for you to calmly say *"No"*, and quickly scoop them up and take them outside or to their indoor bathroom area.

From your sensitive puppy's point of view, yelling or screaming when they make a potty mistake will be understood by your puppy or dog as unstable energy being displayed by the person who is supposed to be their leader. This type of unstable behavior will only teach your puppy to fear and disrespect you.

When you are vigilant, your puppy should not be a difficult puppy to housebreak and they will generally do very well when you start them off with *"puppy pee pads"* that you will move closer and closer to the same door that you always use when taking them outside. This way they will quickly learn to associate going to this door when they need to relieve themselves.

When you pay close attention to your puppy's sleeping, eating, drinking and playing habits, you will quickly learn their body language so that you are able to predict when they might need to relieve themselves.

Your puppy will always need to relieve themselves first thing in the morning, as soon as they wake up from a nap, approximately 20 minutes after they finish eating a meal, after they have finished a play session, and of course, before they go to bed at night.

It's important to have compassion during this house training time in your young puppy's life so that their education will be as stress-free as possible.

Chapter 12: Training Your Boerboel

It's also important to be vigilant because how well you pay attention will minimize the opportunities your puppy may have for making a bathroom mistake in the first place, and the fewer mistakes they make, the sooner your puppy will be house trained.

i) Mistakes Happen
Remember that a dog's sense of smell is at least 2,000 times more sensitive that our human sense of smell.

As a result of your puppy's superior sense of smell, it will be very important to effectively remove all odors from house training accidents, because otherwise, your puppy will be attracted by the smell to the place where they may have had a previous accident, and will want to do their business there again and again.

While there are many products that are supposed to remove odors and stains, many of these are not very effective. You want a professional grade cleaner that will not just mask one odor with another scent; you want a product that will completely neutralize odors.

TIP: go to RemoveUrineOdors.com and order yourself some *"SUN"* and/or *"Max Enzyme"* because these products contain professional-strength odor neutralizers and urine digesters that bind to and completely absorb odors on any type of surface.

2. The Effect of Reward, Punishment and Discipline

Any social animal, whether it is a dog or a human being, requires discipline to function effectively in a group. In simple terms, discipline is nothing but acting in accordance to certain rules. These rules may vary from one family to another but are essential to avoid chaos. Domestic canines must be disciplined in order to be able to function like their own pack, which is you and your family. They must be taught that there is a certain way to behave if they want to survive in this group.

Chapter 12: Training Your Boerboel

In a recently conducted survey, it was observed that dog owners who had well trained dogs were 75% more satisfied than those who had never trained dogs. The two things that we use to teach a dog how to behave are rewards and punishments.

In order to understand which one is better than the other, let us take a look at *Thorndike's theory of learning,* which was established by Dr Edward Thorndike, a noted psychologist. According to him, any behavior that ends in a positive event will be repeated. Similarly, a behavior that ends with a negative event will never be repeated. All training methods we use today are based on this theory. For instance, when your dog performs a certain activity that you approve of, give him a reward. This will make him repeat that activity. Sometimes negative reinforcements may become necessary. However, it is best that a negative reinforcement comes from an outside source. For instance, you may have repeatedly told your dog to stop teasing the cat in your house. However, he continues to disobey you and chases the cat. Eventually the cat will try to defend himself and swipe a claw across his face. This painful gash is the unpleasant event that will prevent your dog from repeating the act.

3. Equipment Required for Training

- Collar and lead: When you are training your Boerboel, use a collar and lead that is not very heavy but sturdy enough to hold him back. The collar and the lead give you that position of authority that will ensure that your dog knows who the leader is.
- Treats: Give your Boerboel loads of treats when you are training it. Keep something that you know is very easy to swallow. A soft treat that your dog can eat immediately is recommended. If you give a dog a hard treat, he will forget what he is being rewarded for by the time he finishes chewing his treat. When you do this, your Boerboel will associate treats with praise and will repeat behavior that helped him earn the treat.

Chapter 12: Training Your Boerboel

4. Basic Commands to Teach your Boerboel

There are some simple things that you must do when you start teaching your Boerboel some basic commands. The most important of all these things is the voice command or the question. Before you train a dog, you must get his attention first. If your Boerboel's mind is on something else and he is busy looking elsewhere, he will never learn anything. When you start training, use the words such as "school" in an excited voice. That will grab his attention and he will walk towards you. Give him a treat and praise him. Repeat this routine a couple of more times. By the third time your dog will understand that paying attention to you will get him a treat. Basically he associates the word "school" with fun. This technique applies to every trick that you will teach your dog.

A dog does not understand our language, so he is only responding to the sounds that you are making and the tone of a particular sound. These sounds are the commands that your dog is responding to. There are a few basic voice commands that all dogs need to know.

a) Teaching your dog to sit
First get your Boerboel's attention and make sure that his lead has been attached. Hold the lead in your left hand and the treat in your right hand. Give him the treat but just allow him to lick it. Do not let him grab it. Now say the word "sit" and slowly raise the treat to the ceiling. As your dog keeps looking at his treat, he will have to bend his knees and sit. When he sits give him a treat and praise him. Make sure that you praise him with a lot of enthusiasm. When a dog hears his owner praise him he feels extremely proud of his accomplishment.

b) Teaching your Boerboel to stay down
When you know what your Boerboel perceives when you give him the down command it becomes very easy for you to teach him to stay down. Usually for dogs, the down position is a submissive state. When you start teaching your Boerboel the

Chapter 12: Training Your Boerboel

down exercise, try not to be too loud or overpowering, as this will make him develop fear or will make him aggressive.

To train your dog to stay down, keep him close to your leg and make him face the same direction as you. Now, hold a treat close to his nose and allow him to sniff it. In a very low tone, whisper the word "down" and keep the treat near his nose. Never allow him to grab the treat. Instead, just keep sliding it away from his nose and he will follow it. Place your left arm on the withers and urge him to move forward. Make sure your push is not too harsh. Gently press him down until he begins to inch towards the treat. As he inches forward, use reinforcing sentences like, "Good boy, I know you can do it" and keep sliding the treat away.

Lower the treat to the level of the floor and he will lower his head too. Now, slide the treat away from him while keeping it on the floor. When your Boerboel sees the treat and hears your positive statements, he will feel motivated to go after the treat.

When he has come to the down position where he is resting on the elbows of the forearms, give him the treat. Make sure you praise him well before you hand over the treat to him. Try to keep your Boerboel in the "down" position for as much time as possible. If you do not startle him or move too quickly, he is likely to stay in that position until you find something new for him to do. The idea is to keep your dog relaxed so that he doesn't feel threatened to let go of the "down" position and run.

c) Teaching your Boerboel to Stay

Whether your Boerboel is in a sitting position or in the down position, it is easy to tell him to maintain that particular position for a long time. This is again done with the help of praise and food. Simply giving your Boerboel treats is not good enough. You must be able to clearly tell your Boerboel what you expect from him.

While you may simply pat him and praise him when he is in the sitting or down position, it is a little different when you need him to stay. For this, you must step in front of your dog and place your

Chapter 12: Training Your Boerboel

toes in front of his. Now hold the treat in front of him in your right hand and say "stay" as you allow him to nibble and lick the treat. Do not release the treat for at least five seconds. After this, step to the side of the dog and release the treat immediately. This will teach your dog that holding himself in one particular position will get him a treat.

The next objective is to help him continue this behavior even when you are at a considerable distance from him. So, for the next few days, add a little distance between you and your Boerboel before you give him the treat. As you are stepping away, face your palm towards your Boerboel as a signal for him to stay. Show him the treat but do not allow him to smell or taste it. Eventually he will realize that as soon as you are back next to him, he will get that treat.

As your dog becomes familiar with the "stay" command, you can increase the distance and the time that you expect him to stay down for. After repeating this, you can be sure that your Boerboel will stay until you go back to him or call him to you. Every time he displays behavior that is correct, be generous in your praise.

You may also use a stopwatch or a clock as a measure of the time that your Boerboel is able to stay. This command is especially necessary when you are showing your Boerboel. If he is able to stay by himself for long periods of time and wait for your call, he is rewarded more obedience points.

Again, you must remember that your dog will stay only until he does not feel too threatened. The moment he hears a loud noise or sees sudden movement, his instinct will kick in. So, when you are teaching him commands such as stay and down, make sure that you take your Boerboel to a quiet and secluded spot where there are no distractions that will get his mind away from the training objective.

d) Teaching your Boerboel to come
The best way to teach your Boerboel to come to you is to tell him that something fun is in order when he comes to you on

Chapter 12: Training Your Boerboel

command. Many owners try to threaten their dogs to come close to them. They may call the dog a couple of times and then use a rough "come" command if he does not obey. When you instill fear in your pet, it is negative reinforcement. Just like Thorndike said, any activity that ends in a negative event is less likely to be repeated.

Instead, turn this into a game. One fun way to teach your Boerboel to come to you is to tell every member of the family to hide in separate rooms with treats in their hand. Then call out to your dog and use commands like "Where are you? "Or "Come on, boy". Initially, your Boerboel will not understand that there are treats waiting for him when he finds the members of your family.

However, he will instinctively try and look for you when he can hear your voice but cannot see you. So keep repeating the command until he actually finds you. When he does, greet him with very loud and obvious praises that he will get excited by. Of course, he will also find the treat waiting for him. As he discovers the rooms that each member of the family are in, let him be greeted in the same enthusiastic manner. This will teach him that the command "where are you" means celebration and fun.

If you have kids at home, this activity will become a lot more fun. As you know, kids simply love to play hide and seek. Now, they get to play this with their large, furry friend. The other advantage of using kids is that you can get them to hide in smaller places like the bathtub. So, your Boerboel will have to work harder to find his treats and enjoy the celebration.

Once he gets used to it, all you need to do is enter a room and say "where are you" and your happy and enthusiastic Boerboel will appear from nowhere to find you. This command is especially useful with lead dogs that need to get to their masters when called. Lead dogs are trained to help visually challenged people. When they are trained in this manner, there are very few instances or rather no instances when the dog is unable to find his master.

e) Teaching the Boerboel to heel

We all have seen enthusiastic dogs that will never stop pulling on the lead when they are out on a walk. This is a habit that needs to be curbed at a very young age. You see, there are several things that may go wrong if you are unable to get your dog to walk beside you calmly without getting too excited. Remember that your Boerboel is a really large dog. It will take just one strong pull for him to break the lead and run off. Sometimes, his pull might even be strong enough to dislocate your entire shoulder.

The command "heel" is meant to get your Boerboel to walk beside you calmly when you take him out. Sometimes, a distraction like a stray cat might get him excited and make him tug hard at the leash. Then, you must be able to get him to heel with a simple voice command.

To begin with, start by holding the loop end of the leash in your right hand. Take the Boerboel close to your left leg and hold the leash closer to the collar with your left hand. With this, you have complete control over your Boerboel. Walk three steps holding the leash a way so that your Boerboel stays completely close to you. When you are done walking three steps, ask your Boerboel to sit and praise him if he has walked without tugging. Try this again. If he continues to walk without tugging, you can increase the number of steps to five. Every time you start walking, give him the command so that he knows what he is responding to. Even after five steps, if he is walking without tugging, allow him to sit and praise him. You must release the lead a little and give him a treat after you have praised him thoroughly. You may increase the number of steps each time you take your Boerboel out for a heeling session. When you are done with the session, all you need to do is say "Ok" and release the tension on the leash. The word "Ok" is a release term whenever you are done with a training session for your Boerboel.

If your dog is one that loves to tug and pull as you are walking, use the brake method. Grab the leash tightly and hold your ground. Do not move until your Boerboel stops pulling and tugging. This is your way of establishing command and telling your Boerboel that you will only go where it you want to go and that he is not appreciated for pulling on the lead.

After he has calmed down, start walking. If he looks at you intently or slows his pace down and remains close to you, praise him and reward him well. In a few weeks, you will have a dog that is able to walk beside you politely without tugging and yanking too much.

The heeling session can be a little stressful on your Boerboel. So, after you have finished your session give him a chance to run around freely or just walk about without being held too close to you. This will help him relax and be calm.

5. Hand Signals

Hand signal training is by far the most useful and efficient training method for every dog. This is because all too often we inundate our canine companions with a great deal of chatter and noise that they really do not understand because English is not their first language. Contrary to what some humans might think, the first language of any dog is a combination of sensing energy and watching body language, which requires no spoken word or sound. Therefore, when we humans take the time to teach our dog hand signals for all their basic commands, we are communicating with them at a level they instinctively understand, plus we are helping them to become a focused follower, as they must watch us to understand what is required of them.

If you teach your puppy hand signals from the beginning, it will be so much easier when your dog becomes a senior and his hearing is affected. That way, you can still easily communicate with your dog by using the hand signals he knows.

a) Hand signal to Come

Come: you can kneel down for this command or stay standing. Open your arms wide like you are hugging a very large tree. This hand signal can be seen from a long distance. When first teaching

Chapter 12: Training Your Boerboel

hand signals to your puppy, always show the hand signal for the command at the same time you say the word. If they are totally ignoring the command, it will be time to incorporate a lunge line, which is a very long leash to help you teach the "Come" command.

Simply attach a 20-foot line to their collar and let them sniff about in a large yard or at your neighborhood park. At your leisure, firmly ask them to "Come" and show the hand signal. If they do not immediately come to you, give a firm tug with the lunge line, so that they understand what you are asking of them.

If they still do not "Come" toward you, simply reel them in until they are in front of you. Then let them wander about again, until you are ready to ask them to "Come". Repeat this process until your puppy responds correctly at least 80% of the time. You can also reinforce the command by giving a treat when they come back to you when asked. Always ask them to "Sit" when they return to you.

b) Hand signal to Sit
Sit: right arm (palm open facing upward) parallel to the floor, and then raise your arm, while bent at the elbow toward your shoulder. Sit is a very simple, yet extremely valuable command for all puppies and dogs. If your dog is not sitting on command, try holding a treat above and slightly behind their head, so that when they look up for it they may automatically sit to see it.

Slowly remove the treats as a reward and replace the treat with a "life reward", such as a chest rub or a scratch behind the ears and your happy smile. If your dog is not particularly treat motivated, lift up and slightly back on the leash when asking them to sit (stand in front of them), and if they still are having difficulties, reach down with your free hand, place it across your dog's back at the place where the back legs join the hip and gently squeeze.

Remember - Do NOT simply push down on your dog's back to force their hind legs to collapse under them as this pressure could harm their spine or leg joints.

c) Hand signal to Stay

Stay: right arm fully extended toward your dog's head, palm open, hand bent up at the wrist. Once your dog is in the "Sit" position, ask them to "Stay" with both the verbal cue and the hand signal.

TIP: if you are right-handed, use your right arm and hand for the signal, and if you are left-handed, use your left arm and hand for the signal. Using your dominant hand will be much more effective because your strongest energy emanates from the palm of your dominant hand. While your dog is sitting and staying, slowly back away from them. If they move from their position, calmly put them back into Sit and ask them to "Stay" again, using both the verbal cue and the hand signal. Continue to practice this until your dog understands that you want them to stay sitting and not move toward you. With all commands, when your dog is just learning, be patient and always reward them with a treat and your happy praise for a job well done.

6. Simple Tricks

When teaching your dog tricks, in order to give them extra incentive, find a treat that they really like, and give the treat as rewards and to help solidify a good performance. Most dogs will be extra attentive during training sessions when they know that they will be rewarded with their favorite treats. If your puppy is less than six months old when you begin teaching them tricks, keep your training sessions short (no more than 5 or 10 minutes) and fun, and as they become adults, you can extend your sessions as they will be able to maintain their focus for longer periods of time.

Chapter 12: Training Your Boerboel

a) Shake a Paw
Who doesn't love a dog that knows how to shake a paw? This is one of the easiest tricks to teach.

TIP: most dogs are naturally either right or left pawed. If you know which paw your dog favors, ask them to shake this paw.

Find a quiet place to practice, without noisy distractions or other pets, and stand or sit in front of your dog. Place them in the sitting position and have a treat in your left hand. Say the command *"Shake"* while putting your right hand behind their left or right paw and pulling the paw gently towards yourself until you are holding their paw in your hand. Immediately praise them and give them the treat. Most dogs will learn the "Shake" trick very quickly, and very soon, once you put out your hand, your dog will immediately lift their paw and put it into your hand, without your assistance or any verbal cue. Practice every day until they are 100% reliable with this trick, and then it will be time to add another trick to their repertoire.

b) Roll Over
You will find that, just like your dog is naturally either right or left pawed, they will also naturally want to roll either to the right or the left side. Take advantage of this by asking your dog to roll to the side they naturally prefer.

Sit with your dog on the floor and put them in a lie down position. Hold a treat in your hand and place it close to their nose without allowing them to grab it, and while they are in the lying position, move the treat to the right or left side of their head so that they have to roll over to get to it. You will very quickly see which side they want to naturally roll to, and once you see this, move the treat to this side. Once they roll over to this side, immediately give them the treat and praise them. You can say the verbal cue *"Over"* while you demonstrate the hand signal motion (moving your right hand in a circular motion) or moving the treat from one side of their head to the other with a half circle motion.

Chapter 12: Training Your Boerboel

Roll Over: moving your right or left arm/hand in a small circular motion, in the direction you wish your dog to roll toward.

c) Sit Pretty

While this trick is a little more complicated, and most dogs pick up on it very quickly, remember that every dog is different so always exercise patience. Find a quiet space with few distractions and sit or stand in front of your dog and ask them to "Sit".

Have a treat nearby (on a countertop or table) and when they sit, use both of your hands to lift up their front paws into the sitting pretty position, while saying the command *"Sit Pretty"*. Help them balance in this position while you praise them and give them the treat. Once your dog can do the balancing part of the trick quite easily without your help, sit or stand in front of your dog while asking them to *"Sit Pretty"* and hold the treat above their head, at the level their nose would be when they sit pretty.

TIP: when first beginning this trick, place your dog beside a wall so they can use the wall to help them balance.

If they attempt to stand on their back legs to get the treat, you may be holding the treat too high, which will encourage them to stand on their back legs to reach it. Go back to the first step and put them back into the *"Sit"* position and again lift their paws while their backside remains on the floor.

Sit Pretty: hold your arm straight, fully extended, over your dog's head with a closed fist. Make this a fun and entertaining time for your dog and practice a few times every day until they can *"Sit Pretty"* on hand signal command every time you ask.

A young puppy should be able to easily learn these basic tricks before they are six months old and when you are patient and make your training sessions short and fun for your dog, they will be eager to learn more

Chapter 12: Training Your Boerboel

7. Overheating

Be very careful when training or walking your dog outside during hot weather, so that you do not allow them to become overheated.

Always carry water with you to help keep them hydrated.

TIP: if your dog has a coat that is darker colored, you can easily help to keep them cooler on hot, sunny days by having them wear a light weight vest that is a lighter color than their own coat.

Remember that smaller dogs e.g. a puppy are close to heated pavement or road surfaces, which means that on a hot, sunny day, they will literally be heated from both the bottom and the top. If the pavement is very hot, do not allow them to walk on it. Instead, take them to a grassy area for their exercise.

8. Weaning the Boerboel from his Food Reward

It is impossible to always carry treats around to give your Boerboel. In addition, you must make sure that he is able to

Chapter 12: Training Your Boerboel

respond solely to your calls and not just the treats. For this you must wean him off the treat that he is so used to.

Treats are great in the beginning when your dog is still unable to understand the command that you are giving him. He must be able to form the right association between a command and the acceptable behavior before you wean him off the treats. This process is gradual and you must never stop the rewards suddenly.

Usually, the dog receives a treat every time he performs a certain task correctly. When he is used to a certain voice command, reduce the number of treats that he gets. Give him his treats only at the end of every exercise session. When he is completely used to this new schedule, you can reduce the number of treats to every other exercise session. While you are weaning him, use a technique called the variable ratio reward system. This is when you mix a reward with praise. Sometimes you can give him both and sometimes you can hold back the treat. This will make your Boerboel respond because he is still hopeful that a treat will come his way. Even if you do not give him a treat a couple of times, this hope will not be lost. However, verbal praise is a must as it is the real reinforcement for your Boerboel. All he needs to know is that his master is proud of him for accomplishing certain goals.

9. The Need for Obedience Classes

Obedience classes are not mandatory. However, they work really well if you need to train your Boerboel for showing. Of course, when you choose to have a Boerboel mainly for showing purposes, you can also enroll in handling classes that will teach you how to handle your dog during the show.

There are several obedience classes that are available for you to enroll your Boerboel on. It is best that you choose a class that is closest to your home to reduce the traveling stress that your Boerboel might experience after a rigorous training session. If you are part of a dog club, you may enquire there for basic obedience classes. These clubs also offer classes that will prepare your Boerboel for competitions. You may also hire local trainers who will come to your home and train your dog for you.

The type of obedience class that you choose depends upon your objective for training your Boerboel. If you are just looking at having a well-trained dog, all you need is to teach him the basic commands. If you are planning to enroll your Boerboel in competitions, you must consider the level that he is competing at. In the initial levels, the basic commands are enough to earn him points. As your dog advances into various levels, you will have to put in more time and energy as these titles are highly acclaimed.

Usually, an obedience class for the earlier stages will last for about eight weeks. It is mandatory for the owner to accompany his Boerboel. These sessions are generally about an hour long. You must also make time to make your Boerboel practice the commands that he learns.

When you make it a point to follow the instructions provided at these classes, you will be able to take home a well-mannered dog that takes interest in the activities that you like. The trainers who teach your dogs in these sessions are highly trained professionals who know what it takes to get the attention of various breeds of dogs. They understand the behavior and the temperament of your dog within minutes of introduction and will be able to create customized sessions that will bring out the best in your beloved canine buddy.

10. Surviving Adolescence

The adolescent period in a young dog's life, between the ages of 6 and 12 months, is the transitional stage of both physical and psychological development when they are physically almost fully grown in size, yet their minds are still developing and they are testing their boundaries and the limits that their human counterparts will endure.

Chapter 12: Training Your Boerboel

This can be a dangerous time in a puppy's life because this is when they start to make decisions on their own which, if they do not receive the leadership they need from their human guardians, can lead to developing unwanted behaviors. Learning how to make decisions on their own would be perfectly normal and desirable if your puppy was living in the wild, amongst a pack of dogs, because learning to make decisions would be necessary for their survival.

However, when living within a human environment, your puppy must always adhere to human rules and it will be up to their human guardians to continue their vigilant, watchful guidance in order to make sure that they do. Many humans are lulled into a false sense of security when their new puppy reaches the age of approximately six months, because the puppy has been well socialized, they have been to puppy classes and long since been house trained.

The real truth is that the serious work is only now beginning and humans and their new puppy could be in for a time of testing that could seriously challenge the relationship and leave the humans wondering if they made the right decision to share their home with a dog. If the human side of the relationship is not prepared for this transitional time in their young dog's life, their patience may be seriously tried, and the relationship of trust and respect that has been previously built can be damaged, and could take considerable time to repair.

While not all adolescent puppies will experience a noticeable adolescent period of craziness, because every puppy is different, most young dogs do commonly exhibit at least some of the usual adolescent behaviors, including reverting to previous puppy behaviors. Some of these adolescent behaviors might include destructive chewing of objects they have previously shown no interest in, selective hearing or ignoring previously learned commands, displaying aggressive behavior, jumping on everyone, barking at everything that moves, or reverting to relieving

Chapter 12: Training Your Boerboel

themselves in the house, even though they were house trained months ago.

Keeping your cool and recognizing these adolescent signs is the first step towards helping to make this transition period easier on your puppy and all family members.

The first step to take that can help keep raging hormones at bay is to spay or neuter your puppy just prior to the onset of adolescence, at around four or five months of age. While spaying or neutering a puppy will not entirely eliminate the adolescent phase, it will certainly help and at the same time will spare your puppy the added strain of both the physical and emotional changes that occur during sexual maturity.

In addition, some female puppies will become extremely aggressive towards other dogs during heat, and non-neutered males may become territorially aggressive and pick fights with other males.

Once your puppy has been spayed or neutered, you will want to become more active with your young dog, both mentally and physically by providing them with continued and more complex disciplined exercises.

This can be accomplished by enrolling your adolescent in a dog whispering session or more advanced training class, which will help them to continue their socialization skills while also developing their brain. Even though it may be more difficult to train during this period, having the assistance of a professional and continuing the experience of ongoing socialization amongst other dogs of a similar size can be invaluable, as this is the time when many young dogs begin to show signs of antisocial behavior with other dogs as well as unknown humans.

When your dog is provided with sufficient daily exercise and continued socialization with unfamiliar dogs, people and places that provide interest and expand their mind, they will be able to transition through the adolescent stage of their life much more seamlessly.

11. The Unruly Adolescent

If your puppy happens to be especially unruly during their adolescent phase, you will need to simply limit their opportunities for making mistakes. For instance, a puppy who is digging up the yard, or chewing up just about anything they can get their teeth on will need to be closely supervised so that you can direct their energy into less harmful pursuits.

It does absolutely no good to yell at your puppy for engaging in behavior you are not happy with, and in fact, yelling or getting angry will only desensitize your young dog from listening to any of your commands. Furthermore, although you may eventually get the results you want, if you yell loud enough, your puppy will then be reacting out of fear, rather than respect, and this will be damaging to your relationship. Displaying calm, yet assertive energy is the ONLY energy that works well to help your adolescent puppy understand what is required of them.

All other human emotions (frustration, anger, impatience, sadness, excitement) are "read" by puppies and dogs as being unstable, and not only will the smart and sensitive dog not understand these emotions, they will not respect you for displaying these types of unstable energies. An extremely rambunctious adolescent dog may need to have their free run of the house curtailed so that they are confined to areas where you can easily supervise them.

Make sure they are within eyesight at all times, so that if they do find an opportunity to make a mistake, you can quickly show them what is permitted and what is not.

Adolescence may also be a time when you might have to insist that your young dog sleeps in their crate with the door closed whenever you cannot supervise, as well as at bedtime so they continue to understand that you have firm rules. In addition, keeping on top of house training is also a good idea during the adolescent period of your puppy's life because some adolescent puppies may become stubborn and forget that they are already house trained.

This means actually taking the time to be involved in the process by leashing up your dog and physically taking them outside whenever they need to relieve themselves. This sort of a routine is also a disciplined exercise that will help to reinforce in your puppy's mind that you are the boss. Too many humans with convenient yards simply do not participate at all in the bathroom routine of their young dogs and thereby miss out on endless opportunities to reinforce who is the boss.

12. Rewarding Unwanted Behavior

Often we make the mistake of accidentally rewarding unwanted behavior. It is very important to recognize that any attention paid to an overly excited, out of control, adolescent puppy, even negative attention, is likely going to be rewarding for your puppy. Therefore, when you engage with an out of control puppy, you end up actually rewarding them, which will encourage them to continue more of this unwanted behavior.

Be aware that chasing after a puppy when they have taken something they are not supposed to have, picking them up when they are barking or showing aggression, pushing them off when they jump on you or other people, or yelling when they refuse to come when called, are all forms of attention that can actually be rewarding for most puppies.

As your dog's guardian, it will be your responsibility to provide calm and consistent structure for your puppy, which will include finding acceptable and safe ways to allow your puppy to vent their energy without being destructive or harmful to property, other dogs, humans, or the actual puppy. Activities that create or encourage an overly excited puppy, such as rough games of tug-

Chapter 12: Training Your Boerboel

o-war, or wild games of chase through the living room, should be immediately curtailed, so that your adolescent puppy learns how to control their energy and play quietly and appropriately without jumping on everyone or engaging in barking or mouthy behavior. Furthermore, if your adolescent puppy displays excited energy simply from being petted by you, your family members or any visitors, you will need to teach yourself, your family and your friends to ignore your puppy until they calm down. Otherwise, you will be teaching your puppy that the touch of humans means excitement. For instance, when you continue to engage with an overly excited puppy, you are rewarding them for out of control behavior and literally teaching them that when they see humans, you want them to display excited energy.

Worse still, once your puppy has learned that humans are a source of excitement, you will then have to work very long and hard to reverse this behavior.

Children are often a source of excitement that can cause an adolescent puppy to be extremely wound up. Do not allow your children to engage with an adolescent puppy unless you are there to supervise and teach the children appropriate and calm ways to interact with the puppy.
In order to keep everyone safe, it is very important that your puppy learns at an early age that neither children nor adults are sources of excitement.

You can help develop the mind of an adolescent dog and the minds of growing children at the same time by teaching children that your puppy needs structured walks and by showing them how to play fetch, search, hide and seek, or how to teach the puppy simple tricks and obedience skills that will be fun and positive interaction for everyone.

13. Giving Up is Not an Option

Too often we humans get frustrated and give up on our dogs when

Chapter 12: Training Your Boerboel

they change from being the cute, cuddly and mostly obedient little puppy they once were, and become all kinds of trouble you never bargained for, as they grow into their adolescent stage. Often, it will be during the confusing adolescent stage of a dog's life that they find themselves abandoned and behind bars as their humans who promised to love and protect them leave their once loved fur friend at the local pound or SPCA.

First of all, not all dogs go through a crazy adolescent period, and secondly, even if they do, please read this section carefully, because you can live through puppy adolescence and come out the other side relatively unscathed and a much more knowledgeable and patient guardian. Congratulations are in order if you've been successful with potty training your young puppy and with teaching them to sleep in their own kennel at night. You've also taught your puppy their first few basic commands, and socialized them with many other dogs, people and places, so you should feel proud of all your accomplishments and the leaps and bounds you and your puppy have accomplished together over the last several months.

Even though your adolescent puppy may be starting to act like a Tasmanian devil, and you may be having second thoughts, now is not the time to give up on them and yourself just because it may seem like someone switched your dog when you weren't looking.

Now is the time to remain calmly consistent and persistent, and to know that you will eventually be able to enjoy the happy rewards of your entire puppy raising diligence. Yes, it can be quite a shock when what used to be your well behaved little darling who never chewed anything they weren't supposed to suddenly takes it into their head eat all the tassels off your Persian rug or chew through a seat belt in your vehicle during the short 15 minutes you were shopping. Even more disconcerting might be when your previously obedient and loving puppy, who always listened to your directions, suddenly appears to have gone deaf and can't remember their name when you call them to follow you inside the

Chapter 12: Training Your Boerboel

house, and instead they take off running after a cat three blocks away. And then, what happened to that quiet little puppy that never appeared to have a mean bone in their body that now spends most of their time at the window barking and growling at everything and everyone passing by?

Welcome to the world of canine adolescence, where it appears that your puppy has turned into some sort of monster and all your previous hard work was for nothing. Of course, this dramatic switch from being the world's best puppy into the monster you can no longer control is not true for all puppies, as every puppy is unique. However, being prepared for the worst will help you ride any impending storm and get you both out the other side where you can enjoy an even closer relationship than you previously had. If you are at the stage with your puppy that you are having great difficulties and wondering if you made the right decision to share your home with a dog, rest assured that puppy adolescence is a normal phase of their development, which can be managed, and which will definitely pass. If you are finding yourself totally overwhelmed, there are many professionals who can provide valuable assistance to help you through this stage of your puppy's development.

For most puppies, adolescence will begin between the ages of five and seven months and this is also the time that you need to be making an appointment at your veterinarian's office to have your puppy spayed or neutered. Although neutering or spaying will not prevent adolescent behavior entirely, it can certainly reduce the intensity of it, as during this period there are hormonal changes occurring that will affect your puppy's behavior.

While it's usually hormones that are the major cause of behavioral changes in your adolescent puppy, there are also physical changes occurring at the same time that you may not be aware of. For instance, your puppy will be going through physical growth spurts which might be causing them some pain, as well as changes related to growth in their brain while your puppy's cerebral cortex becomes more involved in thinking for itself. Usually, during this time of brain growth, a puppy will be trying to make choices for themselves, and may or may not yet be capable of making the right choices. This is why their behavior can appear to be quite erratic.

During the early adolescent period of brain development in your puppy, the signals sometimes get mixed up and rerouted, which can result in the perplexing responses you might notice, when for instance, you ask you puppy to sit and they stare dumbly at you, even though they learned this command months ago.
Don't worry because your previous training will return.

14. Other Activities for your Boerboel

When your Boerboel has been trained to follow the basic commands mentioned above, you will be able to enjoy quality time with him. A well-trained Boerboel knows how to behave himself. So, you can easily include him in several other activities in your life without the fear of him disrupting the flow, causing any damage or injuring himself and others around him.

Once you have mastered the basic control tactics, it becomes very easy for you to handle your Boerboel. Remember that during these training sessions, you have also learnt about the body language of your dog and even he has gained a lot of knowledge about your moods and expectations. This understanding makes it much easier for the two of you to communicate with one another.

Now, you can teach your dog things like helping around the house and even taking care of small responsibilities around your farm or yard. When your Boerboel learns to hand out with you, your life becomes much easier. You need not constantly worry about leaving the Boerboel alone at home or making arrangements for him while you are away. Instead, you can simply take him along. You will see that your Boerboel makes a great, reliable companion.

Chapter 12: Training Your Boerboel

One of the best activities that you can indulge in with your Boerboel is hiking or trekking. He can perform this activity with little or no help from your side. He will need to know simple commands like "heel" "sit" and "stay" for you to be sure that he is safe during each trekking expedition. Your Boerboel will love this activity, as it is great exercise that includes his favorite activities like walking and running.

15. Make Sure He Gets Enough Exercise

Exercise is the most important thing for a Boerboel. Just as exercise is important for you, it is necessary for your Boerboel as well. Here are some benefits of exercising:

• For proper skeletal and muscular development, your Boerboel must be exercised on a regular basis.

• For proper metabolism of the food that you give your Boerboel, getting him proper exercise is mandatory.

• Your Boerboel requires ample space in the outdoors to sprawl and get enough fresh air to grow well.

• A Boerboel will be able to keep himself mentally stimulated and active when he is allowed to run and play outside.

• The chances of your dog becoming aggressive will be reduced to a large extent. Since the negative energy gets redirected with exercise, your Boerboel will be less destructive or aggressive.

• Playing with your Boerboel is the best way to bond with him. Of course, you can save on expensive gym memberships.

The best exercise for a Boerboel is a good, long walk. As you have already read in the earlier chapters, your Boerboel is not exactly an active dog. So you do not have to be too athletic to give your Boerboel the right exercise that is required. You can also plan playing sessions with your Boerboel in your yard. He will love to fetch, but don't expect too much speed from him. He has a humongous body.

A dog as large as the Boerboel should never be over exercised. You must always increase the pace of the exercise for your Boerboel for his own safety. You can start with short walks and increase the length of the walks and the speed of the walks as you continue. You must also never push him too hard to perform tricks, fetch or play with you.

16. Electronic Training Devices

Generally speaking, positive training methods are far more effective than using devices that involve negative stimulation.

Furthermore, unless you are training a dog to hunt badgers or rabbits, using electronic devices is usually an excuse for a lazy human who will not take the time to properly train their dog by teaching them rules and boundaries, which leads to respect and an attentive follower. When you do not provide your dog with a consistent leadership role that teaches your dog to trust, respect and listen to you in all circumstances, you will inevitably experience behavioral issues.

Electronic training devices such as e-collars, spray collars or electronic fencing all rely upon negative, painful or stressful reinforcement, which can easily cause a sensitive dog to become nervous or live a life of fear. For instance, a dog simply cannot understand the principles of "invisible" boundaries, and therefore should never be subjected to the confusion of the punishment that occurs when walking across an invisible line within their own home territory.

Dogs naturally understand the positive training methods of receiving a reward, which is not only much more efficient and effective when teaching boundaries, rewards are far kinder, and create a much stronger bond with your dog.

Chapter 12: Training Your Boerboel

The Truth About Shock Collars

First of all, it would have to be an extremely rare situation in which it would be necessary or recommended that you use a shock collar as these devices are usually only employed in extreme situations. However, for large breeds that could seriously harm someone, sometimes these devices are used. The use of remote, electronic, shock or *"e-collars"* is at best a controversial subject that can quickly escalate into heated arguments. In certain, rare circumstances, and when used correctly, the e-collar can be a helpful training tool that could actually save a dog's life if they are acting out in dangerous ways.

An e-collar would generally be utilized in a circumstance where a larger breed of dog has access to free range over a large property, resulting in difficulties getting their attention from a distance if they become distracted by other animals or smells.

Many dogs that have not been properly trained from a young age also learn that when they are off leash and out of your immediate reach that they can choose to ignore your commands, bark their heads off, terrorize their neighbors or chase wildlife. Generally, e-collars can be effective training tools for working breed, herding, hunting or tracking dogs. In these types of circumstances, a remote training collar can be an effective training device for reinforcing verbal commands from a great distance, such as "Come", "Sit" or "Stay". Finally, electronic collars can be used as a last resort to help teach a dog not to engage in a dangerous behavior that could result in them being seriously harmed or even killed.

Electronic Fencing

Honestly, there are far more reasons not to install an electronic fence as a means of keeping your dog inside your yard, than there are good reasons for considering one. For instance, a dog whose yard is surrounded by an electronic fence can quite easily develop

Chapter 12: Training Your Boerboel

fear, aggression, or both, directed towards what they may believe is the cause of the shock they are receiving.

As a result, installing an electronic fence may cause your dog to become aggressive toward cats, other dogs, other humans, other wildlife, children riding by on bikes or skateboards, the mail carrier, or the dog next door. As well, a dog that receives a fright, or in excitement forgets about the shock they are going to receive, may run through an electronic fence and then be too frightened or stressed to come back home because it means that they must pass through the painful barrier again. Furthermore, it is actually possible that electronic fencing may encourage a dog to escape the yard simply because they associate their yard with pain. This feeling can be reinforced if a dog escapes the electronic yard and then is again punished by the shock when they attempt to come home. Another factor to keep in mind with respect to electronic fencing is that other dogs or teasing children can freely enter the yard and torment or attack your dog, and a thief bent on stealing your dog will be able to do so with ease.

The absolute best way to keep your dog safe in their own yard, while helping to establish your role as guardian and leader, is to be out there with them while they are on leash, and to only permit them freedom in your yard under your close supervision.

Chapter 13: Travelling With Your Boerboel

1) Travelling

Your Boerboel cannot be confined to your home all the time. There are times when it becomes very necessary to travel. For instance, the various trips that have to be made to the vet. There could be times when you have to go out of town and your Boerboel cannot be left back at home. So if he is not prepared for this trip, your Boerboel may feel out of place in a moving vehicle. The trip could be either by car, rail or flight. There are a few tips for preparing your Boerboel to travel by the various modes of transport.

Travel by car

The Boerboel must be prepared to travel by car at a very early age. Although the trips by car may not be frequent, there may be instances once in a while when you have to visit the vet. This is when you need to take your Boerboel by car. If he is not used to riding in a car, the whole drive could be traumatic for the Boerboel. In order to make the ride less traumatic and less troublesome you need to take certain precautions.

If your Boerboel is used to a crate at home, then the same crate may be used to travel in the car. If it were an adult Boerboel, then a bigger vehicle would be required to accommodate your Boerboel. Initially, you can try placing your puppy in a crate while travelling in the car. In case you feel he is not comfortable then he can be placed on the lap of another person while you are driving. This arrangement would be perfect when your Boerboel is just a puppy. However, you need to make alternate arrangements when he grows up to be an adult.

There are safety harnesses especially designed for dogs, which are much like a seat belt that strap your Boerboel to the seat. This

Chapter 13: Travelling With Your Boerboel

shields your Boerboel from getting injured or thrown out when there is a sudden jerk. Never let the Boerboel loose in the vehicle. He may climb over you and pester you, which would be quite distracting while driving and this is very unsafe for you as well as your Boerboel.

If you have planned a long trip, then make sure you carry along some paper towels and some old bath towels. You might have to stop to let the dog relieve himself. This should be followed by cleaning him up and for this you will require the paper towels. If your Boerboel were to suffer from motion sickness, you may need old bath towels to clean him up. In case the weather is warm, then you need to carry water with you to feed your Boerboel.

When the car is parked, make sure not to leave your Boerboel alone since the heat inside the car could be very overpowering when the windows are up. Cars tend to get heated up very quickly, even when parked in shade, when the windows are up. If the windows are kept open, there is always a chance that your Boerboel would hurt himself while trying to get out of the car.

While going on a long trip, make sure that the hotels on the way are dog friendly since many hotels do not allow dogs. Carrying ice with you will be a very good idea if you are travelling in warm weather since you may need it when your Boerboel gets overheated.

Travel by air

There are certain specifications to be followed while travelling with your dog by air. For this you need to make enquiries with the airlines you choose to travel by. There are specifications regarding the size, type and labeling of the crate. To make him feel more comfortable, you should add his favorite toy in his crate. Your Boerboel should not be fed hours before the travel to make sure that his need to relieve himself minimizes.

Chapter 13: Travelling With Your Boerboel

If you are planning a long trip, attaching food and water bowels to the crate is recommended so the airline authorities will be able to feed him in between the trip.

The most important aspect is identification of your pet since you will be travelling in separate sections. There should be an ID tag attached to his crate with your contact information. This would eliminate the risk of getting separated from your dog.

While planning a long trip, the most important item in the agenda will be accommodation. Make sure that the place of your stay is dog friendly. If you end up making arrangements without ensuring whether the hotel is dog friendly, then you may end up without a place to stay if it is against their rules to allow a dog to stay.

Travel abroad

If you plan to travel abroad and choose not to take your Boerboel along, then you will have to make arrangements for him while you are away. The following would be your options:

- Have him to stay with your neighbor while you are away

- Request your friend either to stay at your place or visit your place frequently to monitor and feed your Boerboel

- Put him in a kennel. If you plan to keep your Boerboel in a kennel while you are away, you should make sure well in advance that the kennel is clean and hygienic. Also make sure that there is sufficient space for your dog to play and exercise. Before boarding him in a kennel, make enquiries about the kennel from various sources. Enquire as to how they treat the pets, whether they spend sufficient time with the pets and whether they play with them etc. Your Boerboel is your prized possession. He is your friend and your companion. You need to take extra care as to where you are boarding him while you are away. If you are boarding him in a place like a kennel where he comes into contact with other dogs, you need to be extra cautious. So you need to make special enquiries about the vaccination policy of the kennel. This is very necessary, especially when it concerns the safety of your dog since he comes in contact with other dogs and chances of acquiring infectious diseases are very high.

Identification of your dog

The following are the various options for proper identification of your dog:

a) A simple tag with contact details
These are the simple metal or plastic plaques that you put around your dog's collar. Your dog should were this collar at all times.

b) Micro-Chipping
A microchip implant is a tiny integrated circuit, approximately twice the size of a large grain of rice, enclosed in glass that is implanted under the skin of a dog (or other animal) with a syringe. The chip uses passive Radio Frequency Identification (RFID) technology, and is also known as a PIT tag (Passive Integrated Transponder).

The microchip is usually implanted, without anesthetic, into the scruff of a dog's neck by a veterinarian or shelter. The microchip has no internal power source, which means that they must be read by a scanner or *"interrogator"* which energizes the capacitor in the chip, which then sends radio signals back to the scanner so that the identifying number can be read.

Manufacturers of microchips often donate scanners to animal shelters and veterinarian clinics and hospitals. While many communities are proposing making micro-chipping of all dogs mandatory, such as N. Ireland, and micro-chipping is a requirement for any dogs traveling to the state of Hawaii, many others are not especially pleased with this idea because they believe it's just more big business for little reward.

Chapter 13: Travelling With Your Boerboel

For instance, while approximately one quarter of European dogs have a microchip implant, the idea is definitely lacking in popularity in the United States, where only 5% of dogs are micro-chipped. Even though micro-chipping is used by animal shelters, pounds, animal control officers, breeders and veterinarians in order to help return a higher percentage of lost canines to their owners, some of the resistance to this idea can be explained by inherent problems with the ability of some organizations to correctly read the implants.

As an example, if the scanner is not tuned to the same frequency as the implanted microchip, it will not be read, which renders the process useless. Pet microchips are manufactured with different frequencies, including 125 kHz, 128 kHz and 134.2 kHz. While approximately 98% of the pet microchips in the US use 125 kHz, those in Europe use 134.2 kHz.

In other words, if the facility reading your dog's microchip does not have a compatible scanner, your dog will not be identified and returned to you. Furthermore, what may turn out to be worse than the scanner incompatibility problem could be increasing evidence to indicate that microchips might cause cancer.

In addition, some microchips will migrate inside the dog's body and while they may start out in the dogs neck, they could end up in their leg or some other body part. You will have to weigh information known about microchips, including possible cancer risks, and the odds of losing your dog against whether or not a microchip is something you want to have for your dog.

Whether or not you choose a microchip for your dog, generally the cost ranges between $25 and $50 (£15 and £30) depending on what your veterinarian may charge for this service.

c) Tattooing

Dogs are tattooed to help identify them in case they are lost or stolen and many dog guardians prefer this safe, simple solution to micro-chipping. Tattooing does not require locating a scanner that reads the correct frequency and there are no known side effects.

The tattoo can be the telephone number of the owner or the name of the owner. Because a tattoo is visible, it is immediately recognizable and reported when a lost dog is found, which means that tattooing could easily be the most effective means of identification available. Dog thieves are also less likely to steal a dog that has a permanent, visible form of identification. There are several registries for tattooed dogs, including the National Dog Tattoo Registry in the UK, which has a network of Accredited Tattooists across the UK.

The fee for tattooing and registering a dog for their lifetime is approximately £25. In the United States, the National Dog Registry (NDR) was founded in 1966 and since then, NDR has supervised, directed, conducted, or overseen the tattooing of more than 6 million animals. The cost for tattooing a single dog is approximately $10 plus a one-time registration fee of $45.

Local veterinary clinics do both micro chipping and tattooing. You can contact your veterinarian and breeder for the services. Some vets offer these services at their premises for a very nominal fee. After this make sure to register your dog with a legitimate national database.

2) Finding Your Lost Dog

If your dog goes missing, there are many places you can contact and steps you can take that may help you locate your lost dog, including:

- Retracing your dog's last known location;

- Contacting your friends and neighbors;

- Putting up flyers on telephone poles throughout your neighborhood, with your contact details and a photograph of your dog;

- Calling all local shelters and pounds every day;

Chapter 13: Travelling With Your Boerboel

- Contacting local rescue organizations;

- Contacting your breeder;

- Contacting local schools -- children might have seen your dog in their neighborhood;

- Distributing flyers with a photograph of your dog and your contact details in all neighborhood stores and businesses;

- Contacting all businesses that deal with lost pets;

- Posting a picture on your Facebook or other social media;

- Asking your local radio station for help;

- Advertising in your local newspaper.

Chapter 14: The Health of Your Boerboel

With breeds like the Boerboel, there are several health problems that have been inherited from their ancestors. There are also some diseases like cancer that are common to both people and animals. For most of these diseases, we are well aware of the condition when it comes to human beings. However, there are cases when these diseases might be similar in their symptoms but are extremely different in the cure and their manifestation in the canines. So, treatments vary drastically. The point I am trying to make here is that many owners don't consider their dogs as physiologically different. So, if the dog has a fever, they would probably mix the medicine that they would normally take in that situation. This practice is wrong, as you must, as a rule, take your dog to a vet when he is unwell.

The first step to healthcare for a Boerboel is finding a good vet. Since your Boerboel is a special breed, the vet who will treat him will also need to have special qualifications.

1. Selecting a Vet for Your Boerboel

Usually, pet owners select vets who have the right personality to take care of a breed as large as the Boerboel. While this is a very important quality, the more important thing is that your vet must be easily accessible. In case of an emergency, your vet must be available immediately. The ride to your vet must not take more than 10 to 15 minutes.

The next thing that you will check for is the services that your vet offers. Now some of you may have specialized needs like tattooing or even grooming for your Boerboel. You may also require a vet who is able to provide you with the most sophisticated and advanced pet care products. Of course, these services must be timely and must be able to reach you when you

Chapter 14: The Health of Your Boerboel

want. The responsiveness of your vet and his team to your requests is a very important factor in choosing a certain clinic.

Usually, a vet will have all his/her degrees and certificates on display in his/her waiting room. While these certificates give you basic knowledge of the education that your vet has had, there might be some specialized services that your vet may have to provide for your Boerboel. This will require internships or specialized degrees that will equip your vet to deal with specific problems. For instance, a veterinary cardiologist will specialize in understanding the functions of your Boerboel's heart better than any average vet.

You will need specialized attention for your dog when his condition is critical. Now, most veterinarians will perform routine checkups and even simple surgeries. However, you must look for a vet with more experience and knowledge when the condition that you are addressing is severe.

The next thing that is of great concern is the cost of your vet. If he is too expensive in comparison to other vets in your locality, you may want to look further. Never be shy to discuss costs with your vet. Ultimately, any decision that you take with respect to your dogs care is also bound by certain financial restrictions.

After you have taken all these things into consideration, you can take your puppy for the first visit. This is when you have an opportunity to scrutinize the staff and also the doctor who is dealing with your dog. If you are content with the services that you get, you may continue.

Remember, the vet that you choose for your Boerboel must be the one who takes care of your dog on a regular basis. So, when you choose, choose wisely. Your vet will also become your reliable companion as your dog grows up. So, being able to relate to him and getting along with him also matter when you give the final nod.

Chapter 14: The Health of Your Boerboel

2. Preventive Healthcare for a Boerboel

When you go to a breeder to buy a puppy, he/she will only choose ones that are born from a dam whose disease profile is well known. Most breeders will give you a health certificate to tell you what problems you must look out for in your Boerboel. Just to be sure, you can also visit the vet who treated the dam of your Boerboel puppy to understand the problems that your puppy might have inherited. While the dam may pass on the ability to resist certain diseases, she may also pass on parasites and infections to your puppy. As the first step of preventive health care, you must learn everything possible about the health of the dam.

The next step is to get your Boerboel vaccinated and thus, immunize him from the most probable diseases. There is a schedule that you must follow for these vaccinations for them to be most effective for your Boerboel.

Vaccination schedule for your Boerboel

The best thing to do when you bring your Boerboel home is to have him tested thoroughly by a vet. It is a great idea to start a vaccination program when your puppy is still very young. In the first examination, the general health, the skeletal structure and the teeth of the Boerboel are examined thoroughly. After this, you must fix up regular vaccination schedules that will help maintain the health of your Boerboel.

Most of the vaccinations given to dogs are administered in the form of injections. They must be given only by a vet. It is recommended that you and your vet keep a record of each vaccination to ensure that a schedule is maintained. Most breeders will recommend that you give your Boerboel his first vaccination only after 10 weeks. Usually, the dam passes on antibodies that last for at least 8 weeks. So starting the vaccination schedule after this will help maintain the effect of the naturally passed on anti bodies.

Most often, vaccinations are scheduled at intervals of 15 days or on a 15-day cycle. You must always take the advice provided by your vet as the dosage and the cycle will depend upon the type of vaccination that is being administered to your dog.

The vaccinations provided to puppies are usually meant for viruses. The usual vaccinations provided are for hepatitis, parainfluenza, distemper and parvovirus. Most of these vaccinations that you provide your puppy with will require a booster shot after he is a year old and also once after that. Once you have fixed the schedule with your vet, make sure you stick to it and keep it regular.

3. Common Health Problems with a Boerboel

There are some diseases that are common to the Boerboel. While some of these diseases affect most dog breeds, others are specific to the Boerboel and are acquired through their genes.

Hip Dysplasia

This is a problem that is quite common in large dogs such as the Boerboel. This is a problem of the ball and socket joint of the hip. There are several genetic and environmental factors that have been held responsible for the development of this condition. Research also shows that there is a very complex inheritance pattern for this disorder. There are multiple genes that are responsible for this condition.

This is the most common skeletal problem that has been observed in dogs, especially the large ones like your Boerboel. When a dog has hip dysplasia, his joints are not fully developed. As the dog grows older, the joint deteriorates until the hip joint becomes incapable of functioning.

This condition normally begins when the Boerboel is about four months old. Sometimes the onset of this disease is a little later when the dog develops skeletal issues like osteoarthritis. In this condition, joint inflammations begin to form. These inflammations lead to serious deterioration and disintegration of the joints.

Symptoms:

The symptoms that are observed in a dog with hip dysplasia depend on several conditions like the amount of laxity in the joints, the degree of inflammation of the joints and the duration of the condition in the animal. The most common symptoms include:

- Looseness or laxity in the joints
- Degeneration of the joints
- Reduced activity
- Inability and hesitation while rising
- Hesitation while jumping or using the stairs
- Lameness in the hind limb
- Gait that is swaying
- Keeping the hind legs unnaturally close while standing
- Evident discomfort around the hip joint
- Joint movement accompanied by grating
- Reduced range of motion in the hips
- Reduction in the mass around the quads
- Enlargement of the muscles around the shoulder due to excessive load on the shoulders.

Causes
- Genetic Inheritance
- Obesity
- Lack of Nutrition
- Too much mass in the pelvic region

Diagnosis

Your vet might insist on getting a blood profile of your Boerboel to check for any reduction in the blood count. Since inflammation and joint laxity are important factors in determining the severity of the condition, some physical examinations may also be necessary. X rays are useful in studying the extent of damage caused by the condition. Your doctor may also want to study the parentage of your Boerboel to understand the potential danger of the condition to the functionality and well being of your Boerboel. For this you may have to arrange for an interaction between your breeder and the vet.

Treatment

Usually, Boerboels that have hip dysplasia are treated on an outpatient basis. Surgery is recommended only in severe cases. In the initial stages, exercises like swimming are very useful in controlling the condition. Watching the weight and diet of your Boerboel is also important in controlling the amount of damage possible.

Aortic Stenosis

Aortic Stenosis is a condition that is common in most large dogs. This is a congenital condition, which means that it is present at birth in most dogs. In fact, this is the second most common congenital condition in canines.

Aortic Stenosis is a condition that affects the aortic valve. When the aortic valve starts narrowing, the blood flow from the left ventricle to the aorta is highly affected. This obstruction is called Aortic Stenosis. When this condition occurs, a lot of pressure is put on the heart to pump blood to various parts of the body. As a result, the muscles in the heart enlarge or the muscle cells begin to increase to ensure that the blood flow is normal. Subsequently, the heart wall also begins to thicken, leading to several complications.

Symptoms:

There are three types of Aortic Stenosis:
- Valvular: When the obstruction is present at the valve

- Subvalvular: When the obstruction is present below the valve
- Supervalvular: When the obstruction is present above the valve.

The symptoms that occur are dependent on the type of aortic stenosis that the dog is suffering from. Usually, the defect occurs right at birth. However, the symptoms may appear at any age depending upon the type of stenosis and the severity of the condition. However, there are some common symptoms that you must look out for in case of aortic stenosis:
- Syncope or sudden absence of consciousness
- Dyspnea or uncomfortable breathing
- Congestive Heart Collapse
- Rapid Breathing
- Lung Sounds that are abnormal.

Causes
Usually, aortic stenosis occurs at birth. Sometimes, this condition develops due to bacterial endocarditis. This infection results in a blockage or obstruction in the aortic valve.

Diagnosis:

If your vet suspects aortic stenosis in your dog, he/she may ask to review the entire health history of the dog. This helps determine the onset of the condition and also the severity of the condition in your dog. A complete physical examination is necessary to be sure if there is any irregularity in the functioning of the valve. Even if your dog has significant heart murmurs, it may not be a sign of aortic stenosis. In some cases, it may even occur due to injuries, fever and infection.

Several tests in the laboratory are also necessary to check for the condition and its severity. These tests include a complete blood count, urine analysis, biochemistry profile and several others. Although most of these tests are usually normal for a dog with aortic stenosis, they help rule out the possibility of other causes for the heart murmurs.

Chest X-rays are also necessary as they often reveal the presence of an enlarged heart. In dogs that have congestive heart failure, abnormalities are also found in the lungs of the dog.

In case a more detailed evaluation is necessary, an echocardiography may be performed on the dog. These tests help detect any thickening of the left ventricle wall or the aortic valve. In many dogs, an enlarged aorta may also be observed as a result of the stenosis.

The next step is to check the pressure of the blood flowing through the valve. For this, there are advanced tests like cardiac catheterization. This test involves the insertion of a catheter in the heart chamber or the vessel of the dog.

Treatment

There are several guidelines for the treatment of aortic stenosis. These treatment guidelines vary as per the type of stenosis that your dog is suffering from. Additionally, the vet who is treating your dog also matters when it comes to the type of treatment chosen for your dog. Usually each expert has his/her own preferred method of treating and curing the condition. However, the common goal of any type of treatment is to take care of the complications that arise due to the condition.

In order to cure the condition completely, it is necessary to conduct open-heart surgery. Another option is to replace the valve completely. However, most doctors do not recommend surgeries for dogs, as the prognosis is never favorable.

Catheterization is an option to increase the width of the vessels. However, there are no survival advantages of this procedure when the condition is too severe.

Chapter 14: The Health of Your Boerboel

The most preferred treatment method for a dog with aortic stenosis is giving him broad-spectrum antibiotics as he is constantly at the risk of developing bacterial infections in the heart.

Post Treatment Care

The symptoms of the condition must be reduced in order to improve the life quality of the dog. The activity level of the dog must be reduced to prevent fatal consequences. Special diets, especially those that are low in sodium, are always recommended.

If your dog has been diagnosed with this condition, breeding is not a good option. It is best to have your dog neutered. Keep an eye on the dog and ensure that abnormalities and obvious signs and symptoms are always under control.

Skin problems in the Boerboel

There are several skin problems that affect Boerboels. It is a fact that vets are consulted for skin problems in dogs more than any other recorded condition. Even if you see that the dog is displaying visual symptoms similar to humans, you must never assume that it is the same disorder. There are many creams available in pet stores, although these creams are only useful when it comes to treating the symptoms. If you want to treat the underlying problem, consult a vet. The common skin problems in Boerboels are:

Hereditary skin problems

Sometimes, both the parents of the Boerboel might seem completely normal. However, one or both may carry a recessive gene for a particular skin disorder. If this recessive gene is expressed in the Boerboel, he will display the condition. The most common hereditary skin problems are cuta Boerboelus asthenia, sebaceous adenitis, dermatomytisis and nodular dermatofibrosis.

Most of these skin disorders may also have secondary diseases like cancer and respiratory diseases associated with them. Therefore, it is mandatory to have these conditions checked by veterinarians.

Parasite Bites

When a dog is bitten by a parasite, he may just scratch or bite the area. He will respond to a parasite only when he has been bitten. Most of these parasite bites lead to inflammation of the skin, eruptions and also infections. The sad thing is that before your Boerboel has reached out and scratched the parasite, the damage is already done. Sometimes, the parasite may also have laid eggs that may aggravate the problems in the future. When parasites bite into the skin of the Boerboel, they also leave behind the saliva, which causes itching and irritation.

Auto Immune Skin Problems

These problems occur when the body begins to fight against itself. The most common autoimmune skin problems include lupus, which is common to dogs and humans. Of course, the symptoms are different for people and canines. These autoimmune diseases, if not treated correctly, can lead to the death of your Boerboel. It is not transmissible. These conditions are usually treated with corticosteroids quite effectively.

Acral Lick Dermatitis

This is a condition that affects several breeds of dogs. However, it is quite poorly understood. This condition occurs when a dog licks a particular part of his body again and again. The lick is so intense sometimes that the hair from that region is removed. Since this condition is not known fully, the cure is not known either. It may be controlled to a certain extent using corticosteroids.

Allergies

Just like people, dogs are also prone to air borne allergies. The reaction of the dog when he has an allergen such as pollen on his body is similar to the presence of a parasite. He will bite and scratch that area rigorously. In the process, he may damage the area or cause wounds that are deep and painful.

Food problems in the Boerboel

There are several diseases that are food related. While some of them might be internal, the others might have external causal factors like allergens and toxins that make their way into the dog's stomach through processed, artificial foods that are easily available on stands.

Allergies

There are several foods that dogs are allergic to. You must keep a close watch on your pet when you introduce him to any food group or brand. Sometimes, even the most popular and highly recommended brand may not work well with your Boerboel. It is best to consult your vet if you notice that the problem persists. He/she may be able to identify a certain element that your dog is allergic to. Replacing the food brand that you currently use with a brand that replaces the allergen can yield positive results.

Intolerance

When your Boerboel is unable to digest certain foods, he is said to be intolerant to that particular food. For instance, many dogs may not be able to digest cow's milk. The most common symptoms of food intolerance are stomach pain, passing gas and also eliminating loose stools.

Usually, it is quite hard to diagnose these issues, as the symptoms are very few. With the help of your vet, however, you should be able to find the reason for your Boerboel's discomfort. If the problem is an allergy or intolerance, the best way to deal with it is

Chapter 14: The Health of Your Boerboel

to put your Boerboel on a diet that is recommended by your vet. You can also eliminate elements and food groups that are causing problems. In case of infections and internal issues, your vet will also administer oral medication.

Parasites:

There are two types of parasites that dogs have to deal with: Internal Parasites and External Parasites. Some of these parasites form a symbiotic relationship with the dog and actually promote good health. The problem arises when the parasites that are found on or inside the body result in painful symptoms that do not allow a dog to function normally.

Ectoparasites

The parasites that live on the body of the Boerboel are known as ecto parasites. The most common ectoparasites are:

- Fleas: Every dog owner is familiar with the dreadful problem of fleas. The problem with fleas is that they often multiply at an uncontrollable rate. They also lay eggs that will cause the problem to become prolonged. Fleas are usually a problem during the summer months. As soon as a flea hatches, it needs a host to feed on. Once it has found a host, it will never leave voluntarily. These fleas suck the blood of the host, leaving its skin irritable and itchy. You can control the problem of fleas by using creams and powders to eliminate them after they have grown into adults and to eliminate them in the pre-adult stage. You will also have to clean the sofas, carpets and other possible hiding spots for fleas as well.

- Ticks: they are usually found in tropical and temperate areas. The treatment is similar to the treatment of fleas. However, you must be quicker to deal with ticks, as the damage caused by them is much greater. Ticks tend to harpoon, which means that they dig deep into the skin of the dog to drink the blood. In that process, they also cause diseases like Rocky Mountain Disease, Lynn disease and tick bite paralysis that are severe and difficult to treat.

Chapter 14: The Health of Your Boerboel

- Mites: There are several types of mites that vary in the kind of proboscis or mouth that they have. The best way to keep your dog free from mites is to ensure the complete hygiene of your dog. Mites may affect several parts of your dog's body, including the skin and the ears. The treatment for mites depends upon the type of mite and the area that it has infested.

Endoparasites:

These are parasites that live inside your Boerboel and may cause serious internal damage if not treated immediately. The common internal parasites include:

- Roundworms: These parasites live in the intestines of the dog and are known for shedding many eggs. The biggest issue with round worms is that they also infect humans when they come into contact with them. These parasites cause coughing, vomiting and also bloating in puppies. In younger Boerboels, roundworms are usually transmitted through the dam's milk. In adult dogs, contact feces and also rodents cause roundworm infection.

- Hookworms: There are several species of hookworms that are known to infect dogs. The most dangerous ones are usually found in the warmer regions of the world. Some of them may cause a lot of blood loss for your Boerboel. The only saving grace with these parasites is that they can be treated effectively. When you notice common symptoms like dark stool, weight loss, anemia and also skin problems, have your dog checked for hookworms immediately.

- Tapeworms: Tapeworms are always transmitted by fleas in dogs. While these parasites are not really dangerous for the dogs, they can cause serious damage to us humans. It is possible that the fleas on your dog's fur enter your body through food or through your hands. Then, they release the tapeworms in your body and can cause diseases like alveolar hydatid.

Chapter 14: The Health of Your Boerboel

- Heartworms: These parasites are extremely thin and can grow up to 12 inches in length. These worms live in the dog's heart and affect all the blood vessels and surrounding organs. These worms are transmitted to the dog through mosquitoes. If heartworms are not eliminated, your dog might become anemic. The most obvious symptoms of heartworm infection include fatigue, coughing and lack of appetite.

Ophthalmic Diseases

Dogs are prone to several eye related issues that need to be taken care of at the earliest. Just like humans, the eyes play a vital role in the cognitive functioning of a dog. Any abnormality or problem related to the vision of your pet requires immediate attention and effective treatment for your dog to be active and remain at the peak of his health.

There is no single cause for eye related issues. However, there are some causal factors that are common for all breeds of dogs. Any injury such as a cat scratch is the primary reason for infections and visual issues in dogs. Some infections like conjunctivitis may be caused by bacterial, viral or fungal infections. Such infections might be offshoots of systemic infections or might be localized to the eyes of your Boerboel.

In the case of the Boerboel, all the common eye problems including eyelid conformation problems, glaucoma and retinal degeneration are genetic in origin. Therefore, when you purchase a puppy, make sure that both the parents have been checked thoroughly by a veterinary ophthalmologist and are certified eye disease free.

4. Dental Care for Your Boerboel

Studies show that at least 50% of dogs have some form of gum disease by the time they are three years old. This must be avoided, as dental problems are not localized in dogs. When there is tartar or plaque buildup on the teeth, the bacteria that thrive also enter

Chapter 14: The Health of Your Boerboel

the blood stream of the Boerboel. Some of these bacteria may cause serious damage to the vital organs of your Boerboel.

Therefore, a routine dental check up is mandatory. The first and most important dental visit is when your Boerboel is six months old. This is when the dentist will be able to confirm that your Boerboel has teeth that are fully developed and in good condition. After this, you must fix a schedule for a routine check up and dental maintenance for your Boerboel.

In order to avoid issues like mouth odor and plaque, make sure that you brush your Boerboel's teeth regularly. However, if you observe problems like hesitation to chew, loss of appetite and bad mouth odor, take your pet to the dentist immediately.

Chapter 15: Behavioral Problems in the Boerboel

Sometimes your vet may also have to deal with the psychological issues that your Boerboel faces. The temperament of each dog is formed when he is in his mother's womb. So, we have very little control over that. What we can control, however, is the behavior of the dog. By training him effectively, we can reduce the following behavioral problems:

Aggression

This is a behavioral problem that most pet owners have to deal with. However, when you are dealing with a large dog like the Boerboel, aggression is a big problem as it can become potentially dangerous. When a dog becomes aggressive, he tends to attack people and other animals. This behavior is not just inappropriate; it is also hazardous. Therefore, you must never ignore this behavior.

The earliest signs of aggression are lunging and biting. As your dog becomes more aggressive, he will start growling and even bearing his teeth. This is frightening even for the owner. Usually, dogs show aggression as a sign of dominance. So, the first step is to establish the fact that your dog does not have a dominant role in your household. Next, you must determine if the source of aggression is something else. For this, you must observe the behavior of your dog thoroughly.

When you know that your dog is being aggressive, try your best to avoid provoking him. You must silently observe your dog. If he is trying to project himself as a large animal by putting his chest out and keeping his ears sharp, you must immediately understand that he is trying to assert his dominance. Even if you

Chapter 15: Behavioral Problems in the Boerboel

have the reason for your dog's behavior completely figured out, do not try to solve the issue yourself. An aggressive dog is also unpredictable. Therefore, you need a specialist like a behavioral psychologist to help your Boerboel. If you are unable to control the aggression of our dog effectively, you may have to send him away as he is a hazard to your family.

Usually, aggression manifests in two forms:

- Aggression towards dogs: A Boerboel is aggressive towards another dog for two reasons. The first one is if he has not been exposed to other dogs when he was younger, so he sees another dog as a threat. The other reason is that he is simply trying to assert his dominance.

- Dominant Aggression: Boerboels are alpha dogs. This means that they will want to lead a pack in the absence of a good leader. In the case of the Boerboel, your family is his pack. So, if you do not show him right from the beginning that you are the leader, he will try to take over. The best ways to ensure that you are the leader is to establish that you are the source of food and security right from when he is a puppy. The next thing to do is to train him well and train him consistently so that he gets used to receiving commands from you.

Sexual behavior

Sexual behavior displayed by dogs varies from one individual to another. While some dogs are quite calm even when they are in heat, some of them become overly aggressive when they are ready for the mating season. Usually, in order to curb inappropriate sexual behavior, vets recommend that you have your Boerboel spayed by the time he is 1 year old. Spaying or Neutering has the following advantages:

- Sexual behavior is not prominent. The dogs are usually calm and less aggressive when they are neutered.

Chapter 15: Behavioral Problems in the Boerboel

- Since their hormones are in control, dogs are much easier to train when they have been neutered.
- Diseases like cancer of the testicles may be avoided in adult dogs when they are neutered.

Of course, if you want to enroll your Boerboel in shows or breed your Boerboel, spaying or neutering is not an option. In such cases you must understand the sexual cycle of your Boerboel. For instance, a female has two estruses each year. Every cycle lasts for 3 weeks. In case a bitch is not mated in this season, she will develop false pregnancy. The mammary gland will become enlarged and she will show maternal affection towards all her toys.

In males, mounting is common when they are not mated in the right season. They will mount on just about anything to relieve their sexual tension. Speak to your breeder in order to avoid this sexual tension from manifesting as aggression.

Jumping

Jumping is a dog's favorite way of greeting his owner. While you may be used to it, having a dog the size of a Boerboel jump on them might be unnerving to people who are new to him. So, to keep him well behaved at all times, try to curb this habit. Whenever your dog starts jumping, use a sharp command like "no" or "off" to tell him that you do not appreciate his enthusiasm. Try to force him to sit as you praise him generously. When he does obey you, pet him and feed him a treat.

Digging

If you come home to find several holes in your yard, you know who has done it. It is your Boerboel, of course. Now, digging is a habit that is instinctive for dogs. For a long time, dogs have made holes to look for food or hide their food. So, although we expect

Chapter 15: Behavioral Problems in the Boerboel

the modern lines to have given up this habit, they are still ardent diggers.

In modern dogs, however, the reason for digging is quite different. It is a great pastime for when they are bored out of their minds. So, if you give your dog ample exercise, you might be able to help him drop the habit of digging.

Another easy way to control your Boerboel's digging habit is to provide him with a designated area in your home where he can dig to his heart's content. It is not right for you to cut off an activity that is so instinctive to him. So, the best thing to do would be to redirect his energy and his habit so that he can develop a healthy habit that fits into your lifestyle too.

Barking

Barking is a behavioral problem only when it is incessant and untimely. Your Boerboel is using his bark as a way to protect you. So, you must not really stop your Boerboel from barking altogether. After all, he is a guard dog whose job is to inform you when there is an intruder on your property. So, whether it is a friendly neighbor or an intruder, they are all threats to your Boerboel and you can expect him to bark. This is his way of warning you and ensuring that you know when danger is impending.

So, when does barking become a problem? When your Boerboel barks for no reason at all! Yes, he will indulge in incessant barking if he is not stopped. All he is trying to do is grab your attention. The best way to solve the issue of barking is by understanding the kinds of barks and the message behind them. For instance, the bark of a dog when he sees a squirrel is very different from when he wants food. When you are able to tell this difference, you will be able to cut down on unwanted barking. A barking issue will become very evident at a really young age. If

Chapter 15: Behavioral Problems in the Boerboel

you tell your dog "no" and reward him when he is calm and quiet, he will learn not to bark unnecessarily.

Food begging

The ultimate goal for any dog is to get his hands on the treats that he sees around your home. Some dogs simply steal the food while some dogs beg for food from the table. Both these habits are unacceptable as your Boerboel may get his paws on some food that he is allergic to. There are also some foods like candy that are not good for the dogs and must be avoided at all times.

At a very young age, dogs form this notion that their masters are keeping all the good food for themselves. So they will try every tactic possible to get some of the good food. The habit of begging is triggered by specific stimuli. For instance, when your dog hears the sound of cutlery or dishes just before you sit down to eat, he will stand with his paws in the air, wag his tail and look at you intently for some food.

The only way to curb this habit is by ignoring him. Dogs are clever creatures and will try to whine and cry to guilt you into giving them food. You must ignore the habit as much as you can until it becomes extinct. Instruct all your family members to do the same and discourage bad behavior.

Chapter 15: Behavioral Problems in the Boerboel

Dealing with Behavioral Problems

In order to curb behavioral problems, here are some simple tips that you can follow:

- Never reprimand or punish a dog for wrong behavior.
- Observe his behavior carefully.
- If your dog is displaying bad behavior, do not reward him to change the behavior. He will think of the reward as an incentive for displaying the bad habit. For instance, a dog will be quiet when he is given a treat if he is barking. This, however, makes your dog think that he is being rewarded for barking
- Take the help of a behavioral specialist
- Be extremely patient while dealing with a dog's behavioral problems.

Training from an early age is the only sure shot way of ensuring that your dog is well mannered and well behaved.

Chapter 16: Showing a Boerboel

Showing your dogs in a competition is not just about getting your dog to look good and cute. There are several things that you must do from when your dog is still a puppy. If you have decided that your dog is meant for shows, then training him is crucial. After all, you want your dog to enjoy the process of showing just as much as you and the others present there. Here are some tips to give your dog an advantage over the rest when he is presented at shows:

Socialization is a must

Showmanship is a very important trait among dogs. If your dog is not socialized at a young age, there is no chance that he will make a good show dog. Even if your Boerboel is great at conformation, he will not stand out and shine the way he must if he is not comfortable around people. Each time you take the dog to a new place, he will be unable to perform well as his shyness overpowers his skills. To socialize your dog:

- Take him wherever you go after he has been vaccinated as a puppy.
- Make him aware of various environments. He must be exposed to different surfaces like cement, wood, grass, carpet, rubber etc.
- Take him to new places and allow him to meet new people.
- There are several puppy kindergartens that you can take your Boerboel to. These classes are meant to help your Boerboel socialize with several other dogs and puppies.
- Do not stop people from petting and interacting with your puppy. When he is young, your Boerboel will be more allowing of this than when he is grown up.

Socialization builds confidence in dogs. This is a winning quality that all judges love. Any dog that is comfortable being around people will be able to display all his tricks confidently and will therefore be loved by the crowd as well as all those on the panel.

Attend conformation classes

There are several kennels and clubs that have weekly classes that are directed towards training your dog for conformation. You can enroll yourself and your dog into these classes. These classes are usually conducted by dog handlers who have immense experience with show dogs. If you are a novice in exhibiting, these classes are mandatory for you. You will learn all the basics of showing your dog in a ring. It is also a great way to train your dog to understand what is expected of him when he is a show dog. In these classes, you will learn things like:

- Walking your dog around the ring. This is known as gaiting in show terms.
- Stacking the dog on a table or on the ground for the examination. For a large dog like the Boerboel, stacking is usually done on the ground.
- Helping your dog perform basic patterns like down, back, the L, the triangle etc.

Not all dogs are meant to be show dogs. In case your Boerboel is not among the 'show ring' dogs, you must understand that you are putting a lot of unnecessary pressure on him. When you attend a conformation class, you will be able to seek professional help to decide whether your dog really belongs in the ring or not.

Keep your dog well groomed

The last thing the judges want to see in the ring is a shabby dog. You must make sure that your Boerboel is completely clean before he enters the show ring. This means he must be bathed, combed and free from fleas. Some spot cleaning might be necessary for a dog that is going into the ring. For this, you can get several powders and sprays that act as dry soaps to keep your dog clean. You must try to time your dog's bath close to the show

Chapter 16: Showing a Boerboel

dates. Although it is not recommended to give most dogs a weekly bath, you must at least have him thoroughly cleaned before a show. If you choose to spot bathe him, focus on areas like the face, the undercarriage and his legs.

Trimming

For most Boerboels, trimming the fur on the entire body is not a necessity. However, you may have to 'sculpt' the fur of your dog to ensure that he looks neat and clean for the judges. This makes your dog visually appealing and influences what a judge sees on the outside. Here are some trimming tips for your Boerboel:

- If you feel like his legs are too close together, you can trim the fur around the paws. This gives your dog a good stance by making his paws seem well apart from each other.
- If the excess hair on the head, chin, tail and ears is cut off, a dog looks more youthful. This can be included in your regular grooming sessions.
- There is always a small amount of hair that is present directly in front of the tail. Trimming this hair makes it seem like your dog's tail is placed slightly higher.

Never start first or enter last

When you finally make it to the show ring, your timing is very important. Starting off right in the beginning or entering the ring last is never a good idea. If you have a choice when it comes to your position, try to enter in the middle. This gives you a few advantages:

- You can stack your dog well for exhibition. Last minute cleaning, brushing etc. can be taken care of. If you are first in line, you will be up for examination immediately after you have finished gaiting around the ring.
- If you are the last handler, you will have very little time for a touch up. After examining the dogs thoroughly, the judges usually give the dogs one last look that is the deciding factor.

Chapter 16: Showing a Boerboel

Watch the judge

Watching your judge will give you the advantage of time. It will also make you seem more professional in your approach. When you keep an eye on the judge, you will be able to tell exactly what he is doing in the ring. That way, there is no chance that your dog's faults are revealed to the judge, as you are always alert. When the judge calls you up, you will be able to enter immediately if you are watching. Wasting a judge's time is a bad idea as it reduces the time that your dog gets for the exhibition.

Understand the right gait speed

Perfect conformation is a rarity among dogs. Every dog has a slight fault that you must be aware of as the parent. Usually the problem is in the gait of the dog. It is possible to cover or camouflage this fault by understanding the right pace at which the dog must be gaited. Choose a speed that allows your dog to walk at his best. To understand the right speed, you need to watch his normal gait. Observe the hind legs when he is walking away from you. If you notice that his legs seem weak or that the hocks are leaning towards one another, you can try to walk the dog faster or slower to get a better gait. Similarly, watch the front legs. If you notice that his feet converge, you need to adjust the pace to make it better. When you look at the dog from the side, you should not see the shoulders hunched. They must be relaxed. In addition, the feet must not kick out. The top line should not bounce up and down. When you have achieved all this, you can safely say that your dog has a good gait.

The last thing to do is stay calm. Just make sure that your dog is between you and the judge whenever you are showing him. That way you are not in the way of the judge. You must try to keep yourself calm at all times. Dogs are extremely sensitive to your feelings. If there is any sense of doubt or anxiety in your touch, your dog will feel it instantly and will feel less confident.

Chapter 16: Showing a Boerboel

Once your dog has been trained to do his job, he will do it properly. The idea is to just enjoy the experience of working with your dog as a team. As long as you are focused on that, you have no reason to worry during a show.

Chapter 17: The Cost of Owning a Boerboel

When you bring home a Boerboel, you must be prepared to take on the financial commitments. Here is a list of expenses that you will have to bear in mind when you decide to bring a Boerboel home:

The dog: $2000- $4000/ £1000- 2000

Council registration: $50- 150/ £25- 75

Neutering: $200/ £100

Pet insurance: $60 per month or £30 per month

Micro chipping: $50/ £30

Vaccinations: $50-$70/ £20-£50

Crate: $30-$50/ £15- 30

Toys: $30/ £15 for basics

Ongoing Costs

Food: $60-100/ £30-90 per week

Worming medications: $2.50/ £1.50 per week

Vaccination Boosters: $18 - 25/ £10-12 per shot

Veterinary checks: $100-250/ £50-120 per annum

Pet sitter: $10- 25/ £5-10 per day

It can be difficult to accurately estimate what the cost of owning every dog might be because there are too many variables and unexpected medical problems that might arise that may not otherwise be considered average.

Chapter 17: Cost of Owning a Boerboel

For instance, you may like to buy new collars and leashes every year, the latest toys and gadgets, or the most expensive food for your dog every week that might also not be considered average. However, when thinking about sharing your life with a dog, it's important to consider more than just the daily cost of feeding your dog.

Many people do not think about whether or not they can truly afford to care for a dog before they bring one home, and not being prepared can cause stress and problems later on. Remember that being financially responsible for your dog is a large part of being a good guardian. Beyond the initial investment of purchasing your puppy from a reputable breeder, for most guardians, owning a dog will include the costs associated with the following:

Food
Treats
Pee pads, poop bags, potty patches
Leashes and collars
Safety harnesses
Travel kennels or bags
House training pens
Clothing
Toys
Beds
Professional grooming or equipment
Shampoo and conditioner
Neutering or spaying
Regular veterinary care
Obedience or dog whispering classes
Pet sitting, walking or boarding
Pet insurance
Tattooing
Micro-chipping
Yearly licensing
Unexpected emergencies

Chapter 17: Cost of Owning a Boerboel

As you can see from the list above, there are many variables involved in being a canine guardian that may or may not apply to your particular situation. For instance, depending upon where you shop, what type of food and how much you feed your dog, what sort of veterinarian or grooming care you choose, whether or not you have pet insurance and what types of items you purchase for your dog's well being, the yearly cost of owning a dog could be estimated at anywhere between $700 and $3,000 (£420 and £1,800) per year. Other contributing factors that may have an effect on the overall yearly cost of owning a dog can include the region where you live, the weather, the accessibility of the items you need, your own lifestyle preferences and your dog's age and individual needs.

NOTE: another interesting fact that may influence the overall cost associated with caring for a particular breed of dog is, according to a recent study of 2,000 dogs, closely related to what breed of dog you may be sharing your home with.

According to a recent article written by Sarah Griffiths and published in the Daily Mail on June 13, 2014, there is now a list of the top ten most *"destructive"* purebred dog breeds. This interesting study was carried out in reference to damage a dog may cause by ripping up the carpet, chewing through the fence, destroying the plants in the garden, eating the remote or your most expensive shoes, etc. Of course, all us humans expect some degree of damage from our furry friends during their lifetime, however, sometimes it can be quite a surprisingly large amount when you begin to add up the total amounts spent on cleaning, replacing and repairing damaged property, and the amount can be even higher if your dog becomes involved in destroying the neighbor's property, too.

The prize for the top ten destroyer is awarded to the cute and tiny Chihuahua, with average repair costs totaling $1,468 (£866) over the dog's lifetime, followed by the Dachshund, Dalmatian,

Chapter 17: Cost of Owning a Boerboel

Bulldog, Great Dane, Husky, Beagle, Pointer and German Shepherd. On the other hand, the top ten least destructive breeds include the Staffordshire Bull Terrier, causing a reported $302. (£178) worth of damage over the dog's lifetime, followed by the West Highland White Terrier, Yorkshire Terrier, Spaniel, Whippet, Shih Tzu, Labrador, Jack Russell, Rottweiler and Sheepdog.

NOTE: the more popular a particular breed may be, and the more positive traits a particular breed may enjoy will also make the cost of initially purchasing a puppy from a breeder more costly

Chapter 18: Caring for Aging Dogs

1. What to Be Aware Of

As a result of many modern advances in veterinarian care, improvements in diet and nutrition and general knowledge concerning proper care of our canine companions, our dogs are able to enjoy longer, healthier lives. As such, when caring for our canine companions, we need to be aware of behavioral and physical changes that will affect our dogs as they approach old age.

a) Physiological Changes
As our beloved canine companions enter into their senior years, they may be suffering from very similar, physical aging problems that affect us humans, such as pain, stiffness and arthritis, and inability to control their bowels and bladder. Any of these problems will reduce a dog's willingness to want to exercise.

b) Behavioral Changes
Furthermore, a senior dog may experience behavioral changes resulting from loss of hearing and sight, such as disorientation, fear or startle reactions and overall grumpiness from any number of physical problems that could be causing them pain whenever they move. Just as research and science has improved our human quality of life in our senior years, the same is becoming true for our canine counterparts who are able to benefit from dietary supplements and pharmaceutical products to help them be as comfortable as possible in their senior years. Of course, there will be some inconveniences associated with keeping a dog with advancing years around the home, however, your dog deserves no less than to spend their final days in your loving care after they have unconditionally given you their entire lives.

Chapter 18: Caring for Aging Dogs

c) Geriatric Dogs

Being aware of the changes that are likely occurring in a senior dog will help you to better care for them during their geriatric years. For instance, most dogs will experience hearing loss and visual impairment, and how you help them will depend upon which goes first (hearing or sight). For instance, if a dog's hearing is compromised, then using more hand signals will be helpful. This is also another good reason to teach your dog hand signals when they are young so you can still communicate with your dog when he is a senior and when he is deaf.

Deaf dogs will still be able to hear louder noises and feel vibrations, therefore hand clapping, knocking on walls, doors or furniture, using a loud clicker or stomping your foot on the floor may be a way to get their attention. If a senior dog loses their eyesight, most dogs will still be able to easily navigate their familiar surroundings, and you will only need to be extra watchful on their behalf when taking them to unfamiliar territory.

If they still have their hearing, you will be able to assist your dog with verbal cues and commands. Dogs that have lost both their hearing and their sight will need to be close to you so that they can relax and not feel nervous, and so that you can communicate by touching parts of their body.

Generally speaking, even when a dog becomes blind and/or deaf, their powerful sense of smell is still functioning, which means that they will be able to smell where you are and navigate their environment by using their nose.

d) More Bathroom Breaks

Bathroom breaks may need to become more frequent in older dogs who may lose their ability to hold it for longer periods of time, so be prepared to be more watchful and to offer them opportunities to go outside more frequently during the day. You may also want to place a pee pad near the door, in case they just can't hold it long enough, or if you have not already taught them to go on an indoor potty patch, or pee pad, now may be the time for this alternative bathroom arrangement. A dog who has been house trained for years will feel the shame and upset of not being able to hold it long enough to get to their regular bathroom location, so be kind and do whatever you need to do in order to help them not to have to feel bad about failing bowel or bladder control.

Our beloved canine companions may also begin to show signs of cognitive decline and changes in the way their brain functions, similar to what happens to humans suffering from Alzheimer's, where they start to wander about aimlessly, sometimes during the middle of the night. Make sure that, if this is happening with your dog at nighttime, they cannot accidentally fall down stairs or harm themselves in any way.

Being aware that an aging dog will be experiencing many symptoms that are similar to an aging human will help you to understand how best to keep them safe and as comfortable as possible during this golden time in their lives.

2. How to Make Them Comfortable

a) Regular Checkups
During this time in your dog's life, when their immune systems become weakened and they may be experiencing pain, you will want to get into the habit of taking your senior dog for regular checkups. Take them for a checkup every six months so that early detection of any problems can quickly be attended to and solutions for helping to keep your aging dog comfortable can be provided.

b) No Rough Play
An older dog will not have the same energy or willingness to play that they did when they were younger, therefore, do not allow younger children to rough house with an older dog. Explain to them that the dog is getting older and that as a result they must

learn to be gentle and to leave the dog alone when it may want to rest or sleep.

c) Mild Exercise

Dogs still love going for walks, even when they are getting older and slowing down. Although an older dog will generally have less energy, they still need to exercise and keep moving, and taking them out regularly for shorter or slower walks will keep them healthier and happier long into old age.

d) Best Quality Food

Everyone has heard the saying, *"you are what you eat"* and for a senior dog, what he or she eats is even more important as his or her digestive system may no longer be functioning at peak performance. Therefore, feeding a high quality, protein-based food will be important for a senior dog's continued health.

In addition, if your older dog is overweight, you will want to help them shed excess pounds so that they will not be placing undue stress on their joints or heart. The best way to accomplish this is by feeding smaller quantities of a higher quality food.

e) Clean and Parasite Free

The last thing an aging dog should have to deal with is the misery of itching and scratching, so make sure that you continue to give them regular baths with the appropriate shampoos and conditioners to keep their coat and skin comfortable and free from biting bugs.

f) Plenty of Water

Proper hydration is essential for helping to keep an older dog comfortable. Water is life giving for every creature, so make certain that your aging dog has easy access to plenty of clean, fresh water, which will help to improve their energy and digestion and also prevent dehydration which can add to joint stiffness.

g) Keep Them Warm

Just as older humans feel the cold more, so do older dogs. Keeping your senior warm will help to alleviate some of the pain

Chapter 18: Caring for Aging Dogs

of their joint stiffness or arthritis. Make sure their bed or kennel is not kept in a drafty location and perhaps consider a heated bed for them. Be aware that your aging dog will be more sensitive to extremes in temperature, and it will be up to you to make sure that they are comfortable at all times, which means not too hot and not too cold.

h) Indoor Clothing

We humans tend to wear warmer clothing as we get older, simply because we have more difficulty maintaining a comfortable body temperature and the same will be true of our senior companions. Therefore, while you most likely already have a selection of outdoor clothing appropriate to the climate in which you live, you may not have considered keeping your dog warm while inside the home. Now would be the time to consider doggy t-shirts or sweater clothing options to help keep your aging companion comfortably warm both inside and out.

i) Steps or Stairs

If your dog is allowed to sleep on the human couch or chair, but they are having difficulties getting up there as their joints are becoming stiff and painful, consider buying or making them a set of soft, foam stairs so that they do not have to make the jump to their favorite sleeping place.

j) Comfortable Bed

While most dogs seem to be happy with sleeping on the floor, providing a padded, soft bed will greatly help to relieve sore spots and joint pain in older dogs.

If there is a draft in the home, generally it will be at floor level, therefore, a bed that is raised up off of the floor will be warmer for your senior.

k) More Love and Attention

Last, but not least, make sure that you give your senior lots of love and attention and never leave them alone for long periods of time. When they are not feeling their best, they will want to be with you all that much more because you are their trusted guardian whom they love beyond life itself.

3. What is Euthanasia?

Every veterinarian will have received special training to help provide all incurably ill, injured or aged pets that have come to the end of their natural lives with a humane and gentle death, through a process called *"euthanasia"*. When the time comes, euthanasia, or putting a dog *"to sleep"*, will usually be a two-step process.

First, the veterinarian will inject the dog with a sedative to make them sleepy, calm and comfortable. Secondly, the veterinarian will inject a special drug that will peacefully stop their heart.

These drugs work in such a way that the dog will not experience any awareness whatsoever that their life is ending. What they will experience is very much like what we humans experience when falling asleep under anesthesia during a surgical procedure. Once the second stage drug has been injected, the entire process takes about 10 to 20 seconds, at which time the veterinarian will then check to make certain that the dog's heart has stopped.
There is no suffering with this process, which is a very gentle and humane way to end a dog's suffering and allow them to peacefully pass on.

4. When to Help a Dog Transition

The impending loss of a beloved dog is one of the most painfully difficult and emotionally devastating experiences a canine guardian will ever have to face. For the sake of our faithful companions, because we do not want to prolong their suffering, we humans will have to do our best to look at our dog's situation practically, rather than emotionally, so that we can make the best decision for them.

Chapter 18: Caring for Aging Dogs

They may be suffering from extreme old age and the inability to even walk outside to relieve themselves, and thus having to deal with the indignity of regularly soiling their sleeping area, they may have been diagnosed with an incurable illness that is causing them much pain, or they may have been seriously injured. Whatever the reason for a canine companions suffering, it will be up to their human guardian to calmly guide the end-of-life experience so that any further discomfort and distress can be minimized.

What to Do If You Are Uncertain

In circumstances where it is not entirely clear how much a dog is suffering, it will be helpful to pay close attention to your dog's behavior and keep a daily log or record so that you can know for certain how much of their day is difficult and painful for them, and how much is not. When you keep a daily log, it will be easier to decide if the dog's quality of life has become so poor that it makes better sense to offer them the gift of peacefully going to sleep.

During this time of uncertainty, it will also be very important to discuss with your veterinarian what signs of suffering may be associated with the dog's particular disease or condition, so that you know what to look for. Often a dog may still continue to eat or drink despite being upset, having difficulty breathing, excessively panting, being disoriented or in much pain, and as their caring guardians, we will have to weigh their love of eating against how much they are really suffering in all other aspects of their life.

Obviously, if a canine guardian can clearly see that their beloved companion is suffering throughout their days and nights, it will make sense to help humanely end their suffering by planning a euthanasia procedure. We humans are often tempted to delay the inevitable moment of euthanasia, because we love our dogs so much and cannot bear the anticipation of the intense grief we know will overwhelm us when we must say our final goodbyes to our beloved fur friend. Unfortunately, we may regret that we allowed our dog to suffer too long, and could find ourselves wishing that if only we humans had the same option, to peacefully let go, when we find ourselves in such a stage in our own lives.

5. Grieving a Lost Pet

Some humans do not fully recognize the terrible grief involved in losing a beloved canine friend. There will be many who do not understand the close bond we humans can have with our dogs, which is often unlike any we have with our human counterparts.

Your friends may give you pitying looks and try to cheer you up, but if they have never experienced such a loss themselves, they may also secretly think that you are making too much fuss over "just a dog". For some of us, the loss of a beloved dog is so painful that we decide never to share our lives with another, because we cannot bear the thought of going through the pain of loss again. Expect to feel terribly sad, tearful and yes, depressed because those who are close to their canine companions will feel their loss no less acutely than the loss of a human friend or life partner.

The grieving process can take some time to recover from, and some of us never totally recover. After the loss of a family dog, first you need to take care of yourself by making certain that you keep eating and getting regular sleep, even though you will feel an almost eerie sense of loneliness.

Losing a beloved dog is a shock to the system, which can also affect your concentration and your ability to find joy or want to participate in other activities that may be part of your daily life. During this early grieving time you will need to take extra care while driving or performing tasks that require your concentration as you may find yourself distracted.

If there are other dogs or pets in the home, they will also be grieving the loss of a companion, and may display this by acting depressed, being off their food or showing little interest in play or games. Therefore, you need to help guide your other pets through this grieving process by keeping them busy and interested, taking them for extra walks and spending more time with them. Many people do not wait long enough before attempting to replace a lost pet and will immediately go to the local shelter and rescue a deserving dog. While this may help to distract you from your grieving process, this is not really fair to the new fur member of your family.

Bringing a new pet into a home that is depressed and grieving the loss of a long time canine member may create behavioral problems for the new dog who will be faced with learning all about their new home while also dealing with the unstable, sad energy of the grieving family. A better scenario would be to allow yourself the time to properly grieve by waiting a minimum of one month to allow yourself and your family to feel happier and more stable before deciding upon sharing your home with another dog.

The grieving process will be different for everyone and you will know when the time is right to consider sharing your home with another canine companion.

6. The Rainbow Bridge Poem

"Just this side of heaven is a place called Rainbow Bridge.

*When an animal dies that has been
especially close to someone here,
that pet goes to Rainbow Bridge.
There are meadows and hills for all of our special friends
so they can run and play together.
There is plenty of food, water and sunshine,
and our friends are warm and comfortable.*

Chapter 18: Caring for Aging Dogs

*All the animals who had been ill and old
are restored to health and vigor;
those who were hurt or maimed
are made whole and strong again,
just as we remember them in our dreams
of days and times gone by.
The animals are happy and content,
except for one small thing;
they each miss someone very special to them,
who had to be left behind.*

*They all run and play together,
but the day comes when one suddenly stops
and looks into the distance.
His bright eyes are intent; His eager body quivers.
Suddenly he begins to run from the group,
flying over the green grass,
his legs carrying him faster and faster.*

*You have been spotted,
and when you and your special friend finally meet,
you cling together in joyous reunion,
never to be parted again.
The happy kisses rain upon your face;
your hands again caress the beloved head,
 and you look once more into the trusting eyes
of your pet, so long gone from your life
but never absent from your heart.*

*Then you cross Rainbow Bridge together...."
www.rainbowbridge.com*

- Author unknown

Conclusion

Getting a pet home is a real commitment. Unless you are entirely ready, think about it, discuss it with your family and then bring your Boerboel home.

In the end, the most important thing to know is whether a Boerboel is the right dog for you or not. There are some obvious things that will help you make this vital decision. Here is a list of pros and cons of having a Boerboel in your home:

Pros:

- They are great companions
- They are the best work dogs
- Grooming needs are not many
- They are even tempered
- They are good for homes with children and other pets
- They are loyal and protective
- They are easy to train
- They are excellent show dogs

Cons:
- May be dangerous if not trained well
- They are really large
- They are not suitable for first time owners
- Highly attention seeking
- Expensive to maintain
- They need a single master to command them
- Dominant by nature

Conclusion

Once you have considered these pros and cons, you may step right up to a breeder and bring home your gorgeous Boerboel. I do hope that this book has been adequate in providing you with all the information you need about the Boerboel. All the research for this book is based on personal accounts and insights by experts who have a great deal of experience with the Boerboel. I hope you enjoyed this book.

Published by IMB Publishing 2014

Copyright and Trademarks. This publication is Copyright 2014 by IMB Publishing. All products, publications, software and services mentioned and recommended in this publication are protected by trademarks. In such instance, all trademarks & copyright belong to the respective owners. All rights reserved. No part of this book may be reproduced or transferred in any form or by any means, graphic, electronic, or mechanical, including photocopying, recording, taping, or by any information storage retrieval system, without the written permission of the author. Pictures used in this book are either royalty free pictures bought from stock-photo websites or have the source mentioned underneath the picture.

Disclaimer and Legal Notice. This product is not legal or medical advice and should not be interpreted in that manner. You need to do your own due-diligence to determine if the content of this product is right for you. The author and the affiliates of this product are not liable for any damages or losses associated with the content in this product. While every attempt has been made to verify the information shared in this publication, neither the author nor the affiliates assume any responsibility for errors, omissions or contrary interpretation of the subject matter herein. Any perceived slights to any specific person(s) or organization(s) are purely unintentional. We have no control over the nature, content and availability of the web sites listed in this book. The inclusion of any web site links does not necessarily imply a recommendation or endorse the views expressed within them. IMB Publishing takes no responsibility for, and will not be liable for, the websites being temporarily unavailable or being removed from the Internet. The accuracy and completeness of information provided herein and opinions stated herein are not guaranteed or warranted to produce any particular results, and the advice and strategies, contained herein may not be suitable for every individual. The author shall not be liable for any loss incurred as a consequence of the use and application, directly or indirectly, of any information presented in this work. This publication is designed to provide information in regard to the subject matter covered. The information included in this book has been compiled to give an overview of the subjects and detail some of the symptoms, treatments etc. that are available to canines with these conditions. It is not intended to give medical advice. For a firm diagnosis of your dog's condition, and for a treatment plan suitable for you, you should consult your veterinarian or consultant. The writer of this book and the publisher are not responsible for any damages or negative consequences following any of the treatments or methods highlighted in this book. Website links are for informational purposes only and should not be seen as a personal endorsement; the same applies to the products detailed in this book. The reader should also be aware that although the web links included were correct at the time of writing, they may become out of date in the future.

www.ingramcontent.com/pod-product-compliance
Lightning Source LLC
Chambersburg PA
CBHW060824050426
42453CB00008B/578